2~
W9-AGW-130

Ground Covers for the Midwest

T. B. Voigt

Betty R. Hamilton

F. A. Giles

University of Illinois
at Urbana-Champaign
College of Agriculture

Special Publication 65

T. B. Voigt and Betty R. Hamilton are former graduate students in ornamental horticulture and F. A. Giles is associate professor of horticulture at the University of Illinois at Urbana-Champaign.

This book was set in Palatino and Malibu typefaces and printed on Patina Matte paper. Edited by Richard Moores; designed by Joan Zagorski and Doris Kogan; drawings by F.A. Giles. Composed, printed, and bound by the University of Illinois Printing Division, Champaign, Illinois.

© 1983
By the Board of Trustees of the University of Illinois.
Manufactured in the United States of America.

6M—4-83—52814—RGM

Preface

Ground covers are a large, variable group of plants that range from 1 inch to 4 feet in height. Their native habitats include sandy banks, rocky slopes, densely canopied woodlands, and wet stream banks. Some ground-cover plants can be used in refined landscape areas; others are more suitable for rugged, naturalized sites.

Ground covers help to unify unrelated landscape elements, define or emphasize certain areas or features, "soften" harsh walls and embankments, and control soil erosion on slopes. They may also reduce maintenance, especially in areas that are difficult to mow, such as small courtyards, narrow strips between walks and structures, and around patios. When grown beneath trees and shrubs, ground covers protect these plants from injury by eliminating the need to mow around them. Dense beds of ground-cover plants can serve as living mulch, shading and cooling the soil and preventing the germination of weed seeds.

For many years, turfgrasses have been the most widely used ground covers in the Midwest because of their dense, uniform growth and ability to withstand foot traffic. In certain landscape areas, however, other ground covers are more effective. Many of the plants described in this book survive in areas where turfgrasses grow poorly or not at all, and their showy flowers, fruits, foliage, unusual growth habits, and textures contrast pleasingly with other landscape elements.

Although written primarily for home gardeners, **Ground Covers for the Midwest** may be equally useful to nursery or garden center operators, landscape contractors and architects, teachers, and students. It is divided into two main sections: (1) an introductory section containing general cultural information; and (2) detailed descriptions of many woody and herbaceous ground-cover plants, including the botanical, common, and obsolete names of each plant, the hardiness zone in which the plant grows best, and the uses of the plant in the home landscape. Each description is accompanied by line drawings of the leaves, stems, flowers, or fruits of the plant. The book also contains 80 full-color photographs of ground-cover plants, an illustrated glossary of botanical terms, a list of publications for further reference, and an index of botanical and common names. The English system of weights and measures is used throughout because many home gardeners have not yet adopted the metric system.

Many people helped in the preparation of this book. The authors particularly wish to thank the following: Professors William L. George, Jr., William R. Nelson, Jr., David L. Sanford, Donald C. Saupe, and David J. Williams of the University of Illinois at Urbana-Champaign; the late William Cunningham, Cunningham Gardens, Waldron, Indiana; Jesse Felix, Cantigny, Wheaton, Illinois; Peter Orum, Midwest Ground Covers, St. Charles, Illinois; Rodney Raker, Kingwood Nurseries, Inc., Madison, Ohio; John Swisher, Morton Arboretum, Lisle, Illinois; and especially, Kenneth R. Robertson of the State Natural History Survey and Floyd Swink of the Morton Arboretum for their careful review of the manuscript. *Hortus Third* (Macmillan Publishing Company, New York, 1978) was used as the final authority for the nomenclature of the plants described here.

T.B. Voigt

Betty R. Hamilton

F.A. Giles

Contents

Growing Ground Covers

Types of Ground Covers

Ground covers consist of **woody** and **herbaceous** plants. Woody plants have above-ground portions that "harden off." The above-ground portions (which may or may not lose their leaves) and the roots remain alive in a dormant state throughout the winter. Some ground covers help to control soil erosion; others brighten the winter landscape with their colorful stems and persistent fruits. Many are exceptionally hardy, well able to withstand the extremes of Midwestern winters. Both the woody and herbaceous ground-cover plants are perennials.

Woody ground covers may be **deciduous** or **evergreen.** Deciduous plants drop all of their leaves in the fall and grow new ones in the spring. Several of these plants produce leaves that turn bright colors in the autumn. The evergreen plants retain most of their leaves throughout the year.

The deciduous ground covers include upright, shrubby types (*Forsythia viridissima* 'Bronxensis' — Bronx Greenstem Forsythia); dense thicket-formers (*Comptonia peregrina* — Sweetfern); and low, spreading forms (*Rhus aromatica* 'Gro-Low' — Gro-Low Fragrant Sumac). The evergreen ground covers, which provide year-round color in areas of high visibility, may be either **broadleaved** or **narrowleaved.**

Broadleaved evergreens have flattened, leathery leaves that resemble those of deciduous plants. They include vining forms (*Hedera helix* — English Ivy); low, spreading types (*Arctostaphylos uva-ursi* — Bearberry); low clump-formers (*Mahonia repens* — Creeping Mahonia); and mounding shrubs (*Euonymus fortunei* var. *vegeta* — Bigleaf Wintercreeper). The proper siting of broadleaved evergreens is especially important in the Midwest. These plants are susceptible to drying, and should be planted out of winter sun and wind or protected with temporary screens, mulches, or antitranspirants.

The narrowleaved evergreens have fine-textured, scalelike or awl-shaped (needlelike) leaves, and are less susceptible to the drying effects of winter sun and wind than the broadleaved evergreens. This group includes some of the low-growing and spreading junipers; several of these evergreens will also cascade over walls or embankments.

Herbaceous plants usually have soft, fleshy stems. Their above-ground portions commonly die to the ground each winter and regrow in the spring from persistent roots. Ground covers classified as herbaceous do not necessarily leave the ground bare in winter. Some of them are evergreen or develop somewhat woody stems with age; others carpet the ground with their dried stems and foliage.

The herbaceous ground covers include matlike, creeping types (*Veronica repens* — Creeping Speedwell); mounded, small, shrublike plants (*Iberis sempervirens* — Evergreen Candytuft); clump-formers (*Alchemilla vulgaris* — Lady's-Mantle); and vinelike forms (*Lamiastrum galeobdolon* — Yellow Archangel).

Several of the woody and herbaceous plants described in this book are **semievergreen,** and retain their leaves when grown in protected sites or during mild winters. During cold winters or when grown in open, exposed areas, however, they may drop their leaves. The leaves will regrow the following spring.

Selecting Ground Covers

The plant descriptions, drawings, and photographs in this book will help you to choose the proper ground-cover plants for your landscape. In selecting a ground cover, be sure that it is suitable for the use for which it has been chosen. The wrong choice will result in poor visual quality and possibly the death of the plant. Although many of these plants are quite adaptable, others require special care and siting.

First, consider the plant's appearance and rate of growth. Do the color, texture, and form of the plant harmonize with or distract from the existing landscape? Will the plant become too large and quickly grow out of bounds? How rapidly do you want the area to be filled? Plants that cover quickly may soon overgrow their boundaries and become maintenance problems.

Second, consider the plant's cold hardiness (see **Hardiness,** page 10). For exposed areas, you will want to choose plants that are sufficiently cold-hardy for your region. In courtyards and other protected sites, however, broadleaved evergreens and more tender plants may survive with a little extra care, even though they are only marginally hardy for your region.

Third, consider the actual location of the ground-cover bed. Is the site wet or dry, exposed to strong winds, sunbaked or densely shady? There are ground covers available that are adapted to every site and condition. You should

3

also know the pH of your soil. Certain plants tolerate only a narrow pH range.

Finally, consider the amount of care that the plant should receive. Ground-cover plants that are properly selected for a particular site often need little care except for occasional pruning, fertilization, and water; however, some plants require more attention than others. If you do not have time to garden or do not enjoy gardening, you should choose plants that require the least amount of maintenance.

Soil pH, Drainage, and Fertility

Soil pH refers to the acidity or alkalinity of the soil, and is measured on a scale of 1 to 14. On this scale, the lower end (1 to 6.9) is acidic, the upper end (7.1 to 14) is alkaline, and 7 is neutral. A pH of 4 is strongly acidic, while a pH of 6.5 is weakly acidic; a pH of 11 is strongly alkaline, and a pH of 7.5 is weakly alkaline. Knowing the pH of the planting-bed soil is important because most ground-cover plants grow best within a certain pH range (usually between 6 and 7). A soil test will indicate the pH of your soil.

Good soil structure is essential for proper root growth and successful establishment of the plants. A simple test for soil structure is to squeeze a handful of moist (but not wet) soil and then open your hand. If the soil holds together for a few seconds before falling apart into a crumbly mixture, the soil has good structure. If the soil does not adhere and flows through your fingers, it contains large amounts of sand. Sandy soils have many large air spaces that drain quickly. These soils do not readily retain water, and nutrients are easily leached through them.

If the handful of soil forms a solid lump, it probably contains a great deal of clay. A clay soil is composed of very fine particles and numerous tiny air spaces that fill with and hold water. Soils with large amounts of clay are gummy when wet and bricklike when dry.

Soils can often be improved by adding well-rotted organic matter (peat moss, leaf mold, compost, manure, etc.). Very heavy clay soils may be further improved by adding sand. Many of the ground-cover plants described in this book require a moist, well-drained soil. Organic matter increases the moisture-holding capacity of sandy soils. Large, coarse particles of compost make clay soil more porous, resulting in better drainage.

Soil fertility depends upon the amount and availability of the mineral elements necessary for plant growth. Sandy soils usually have lower fertility levels than clay soils. Compost has the ability to hold minerals and moisture in the root zone, where they are available to the plant. It also supplies certain nutrients as it decomposes, an added advantage when using compost as a soil amendment. A soil test will determine if any necessary mineral elements are lacking in your soil. Your county Extension adviser can interpret the test results and recommend the kinds and amounts of fertilizers to be applied and the method of application.

Collecting Samples for a Soil Test

Before preparing the planting bed, it is desirable to have your soil tested. Samples should be taken when the soil temperature is above 50° F., preferably in late October or early November. Collect several soil samples from well-distributed locations in each area in which the ground covers will be planted. The soil must be dry enough so that it does not form a clump when pressed in the hand. Do not take samples after a recent lime or fertilizer application.

Samples may be collected with a soil probe, or by inserting a spade deeply into the ground and taking a vertical core or slice of the soil that is spaded. Discard roots and debris. This vertical core should be about ½ inch thick, 1 inch wide, and 6 to 8 inches deep.

After you have collected all of the samples from one area, air dry the soil and mix thoroughly. Enclose the sample in a sack and pack in a sturdy container. Mail the sample to an approved soil-testing laboratory (a small fee is involved). Be sure to provide at least ½ pint of soil per area, along with information about the intended use of the area and your name and address. The test results indicate the amounts of lime and fertilizer that should be applied. Your county Extension adviser can give you additional information about the soil test.

Preparing the Planting Bed

Proper preparation of the planting bed is important in growing plants successfully. Following the steps described below will make maintenance easier and save you the trouble and expense of replanting a bed that has not succeeded.

The first step is to lay out the bed's outline on the ground. Use string and stakes for straight lines and a garden hose for gently curving edges.

The second step is to remove unwanted vegetation from the planting bed by stripping the soil surface with a square-edged spade. Discard all of the root pieces of perennial weeds. Small portions of these weeds will send up shoots that compete with the ground-cover plants. Perennial weeds are difficult to remove after the bed has been planted. If you have large planting beds, you may also want to consider the use of herbicides (see **Controlling Weeds,** page 8).

The third step in preparing the planting bed is to turn the soil to a depth of 8 to 12 inches either by hand or with a power tiller. Remove any debris or large rocks. If the soil contains a great deal of clay, discard this soil and replace it with topsoil. Improve poor drainage by placing drain tiles 18 inches below the surface of the bed. These tiles should drain into a catch basin or drainage ditch. You can also improve drainage by raising the planting beds above ground level in accordance with a landscape plan or by integrating them into the landscape. Raised beds should not be placed haphazardly in the landscape.

Gravel in the bottom of the planting hole will not improve soil drainage, and may eventually fill with water and form a basin. It will also partially prevent subsurface ground moisture from moving up into the root zone during dry periods.

After you have turned the soil, add fertilizer and any materials necessary to improve soil pH and fertility (as indicated by the soil test). Most soils are also improved by adding at least 3 inches of compost or mulch. Mix all of these materials uniformly to a depth of 12 inches and smooth the bed.

Wait at least 2 weeks before planting to allow the bed to settle and to give any exposed weed seeds a chance to germinate. The weed seedlings can be easily removed.

The final step in preparing a planting bed is adding mulch (see **Mulching,** page 7). The plants will be planted through the mulch.

Planting

It is best to plant ground covers in the spring, when the weather is cool and moist. The plants then have an entire growing season to become established and develop the strong root systems necessary to survive the extremes of a Midwestern winter. If you must plant in the fall, plant as early as possible, and keep the planting watered until the ground freezes. A winter mulch may be helpful (see **Winter Protection**, page 7).

Before planting, determine the number of square feet in the planting bed and the spacing between the plants. Each plant description in this book includes spacing information, but circum-

stances may dictate changes. Large container-grown plants or clumps of ground covers usually cover an area faster than small, individual plants, and may be spaced farther apart than commonly recommended. Plants that grow rapidly can be spaced farther apart than slow-growing plants. Plants on slopes should be grown closer together to shorten the time required to cover. For quick coverage, space plants closer together on level ground. Finally, cost can influence spacing. The closer together the plants, the larger the number of plants required and the higher the cost.

Use the table below to determine the number of plants needed to cover your planting bed. First, find the spacing you have chosen in the lefthand column. Next, divide the number of square feet in your planting bed by the appropriate number in the righthand column. The resulting figure is the number of ground-cover plants required to cover the bed at the spacing you have chosen.

Spacing
(inches)

4	0.11
6	0.25
8	0.44
10	0.70
12	1.00
15	1.56
18	2.25
24	4.00
30	6.25
36	9.00
48	16.00
60	25.00

For example, your planting bed is 23 feet long by 10 feet wide (230 square feet), and you have decided to plant *Hedera helix* (English Ivy) spaced 15 inches apart. The number in the righthand column opposite "15 inches" is 1.56. Divide 230 (the number of square feet in the planting bed) by 1.56 (230 ÷ 1.56 = 147). You will need 147 English Ivy plants spaced 15 inches apart to cover a bed 230 feet square.

Distribute the plants equally to cover the area. Use a checkboard or diamond planting pattern.

Ground covers may be purchased as **seeds** or as **bare-root, balled-and-burlapped,** or **container-grown plants.**

Many herbaceous ground covers are available as seeds. Purchase seeds from a reputable producer who offers seeds that are clean, disease-free, and true to name. Seed-produced plants will not be identical with their parents because of genetic differences, but most of the offspring will become excellent ground-cover plants if the seed is true to name.

Several growing seasons may be required before ground-cover plants produced from seeds are large enough to be placed in the landscape. After the plants germinate, they can be grown in containers or nursery beds until they are large enough to be transplanted into their final bed. When transplanting, handle these transplants as container-grown or bare-root plants.

Bare-root plants or bare-root crowns are grown in fields. These plants are dug when they are dormant, and the soil is removed from their roots. To prolong storage life, the roots are often covered with damp peat moss or sawdust and then wrapped with plastic. Bare-root plants usually cost less than balled-and-burlapped or container-grown plants but require more care after they are planted. Transplant bare-root plants only in the spring when the plants are dormant and the weather is cool and moist. Before planting, remove the packaging and carefully examine the root system. Prune any broken or damaged roots, and soak the roots in water for 24 hours. Place the plants in a cool, shaded area until you are able to plant them. Plant as soon as possible.

Dig a hole through the mulch that is large enough to spread the roots out and deep enough so that the plant can be placed at the same level at which it was growing originally. Make a mound in the center of the hole and place the roots around it. Be sure that the plant is not leaning.

There are two methods of **backfilling** a hole. The first method is to fill the hole with soil and firm the soil around the roots to remove large air pockets. In the second method (the ''slurry method''), water and soil are placed in the hole at the same time. Both methods work equally well.

After backfilling, form a saucer of soil around the plant to capture water and direct it toward the root system. Water the plant well immediately after planting and until it is established.

Bare-root woody plants require pruning after transplanting. First, remove any broken or damaged branches; then eliminate additional growth until you have reduced the number of branches by ⅓ to ½. Use correct pruning techniques (see **Pruning**, page 9). Never leave stubs.

Balled-and-burlapped plants are usually more expensive than bare-root plants. They are grown in fields and then dug, leaving soil around the roots. The root ball is wrapped with burlap and tied with twine.

Dig the planting hole about 6 inches larger than the diameter of the ball and about the same depth as the ball is high. Position the plant carefully in the hole, moving the plant by the ball. Do not drop or break the root ball — you may damage the roots. Set the plant at the same level at which it was growing originally, and make sure that it is not leaning. When the plant is properly positioned, cut the twine that encircles the base of the plant and the root ball. If this twine is left in place, it will girdle the plant and eventually kill it. Fold back the burlap on top of the ball into the hole; otherwise, the burlap forms a ''wick'' and causes drying from the bottom of the plant ball. Backfill, using one of the methods described earlier. Construct a small mound around the plant and water deeply. Balled-and-burlapped plants should be pruned to compensate for the roots that were lost during transplanting.

Container-grown plants may be expensive, but they transplant well because the roots have grown while the plants were in the containers. Container-grown plants can be transplanted anytime if adequate water is available.

Dig the planting hole slightly larger than the container. Remove the plant if the container is plastic or metal. If the container is a fiber pot, remove it completely. Check the root system. If the roots are dense and encircling, make 3 or 4 vertical cuts into the container soil and roots. These cuts cause the roots to branch and eliminate root circling.

Position the plant in the hole, placing it at the same level at which it was originally growing in the container. Make sure that the plant is not leaning. Backfill, place a mound around the plant, and water well. Prune any broken or damaged branches. It is not necessary to prune the top so that it balances with the root system because the root system has not been reduced during transplanting. Container-grown plants may require some maintenance.

Landscape designs often require the planting of shade-loving ground covers beneath trees and shrubs. If the trees are small, they may not provide enough shade for a healthy ground-cover stand. To eliminate this problem, increase the bed size in stages, starting with small beds and enlarging them as the trees grow.

Planting ground covers on slopes presents special problems because erosion removes the topsoil, making it difficult for the plants to become established. Following the practices described below will allow you to grow ground covers successfully on slopes.

First, apply a mulch. Mulches help the plants to become established by keeping the soil cool and moist. They also protect the soil surface from erosion until the plants cover completely. Second, to prevent the loose soil surface from eroding, dig holes only for the individual plants instead of tilling the entire slope. Third, select plants that are well-suited for growing on slopes. The plants should be vigorous spreaders that form roots at various points along their spreading stems. Junipers grow well on slopes, but they do not prevent the soil from eroding because they rarely root along their long stems. Finally, space the plants closer together on slopes. To reduce erosion, plant in a diamond pattern in rows that run perpendicular to the slope. On severe slopes, you may need to construct terraces to provide flattened areas for planting.

Mulching

Apply mulch to your ground-cover beds before planting. Organic and inorganic mulches inhibit the growth of weeds, moderate soil temperatures, conserve soil moisture, reduce erosion, prevent crusting or drying of the soil surface, and decrease frost heaving. As organic mulches slowly decompose and become incorporated into the soil as humus, they release plant nutrients. They also give the beds a pleasing, natural appearance.

Do not apply mulch so thickly that air and water are kept from the soil. Apply 1 to 2 inches of a fine-textured mulch for small, more delicate, and very low-growing plants, and 2 to 4 inches for larger and shrublike plants. Coarser textured mulches may also be used with bigger plants. Do not bring the mulch up to the base of the plant; leave a small, clear area to reduce the possibility of damage from rodents and diseases. Moist mulch around the bases of many herbaceous ground covers will cause stem and crown rot.

Mulching materials should be weed-free, nonmatting, easy to apply, and readily available. Ground corncobs, bark chunks, mushroom compost, pecan hulls, and composted wood chips or sawdust are all suitable organic mulching materials. Do not use fresh wood products. As these products are decomposed by microorganisms, they compete with the plants for nitrogen. Peat moss is not a suitable mulching material because it is difficult to wet and may blow away when dry.

Do not use plastic film or sheeting for ground-cover beds. Many ground covers spread by sending up shoots from the roots or by the rooting of spreading stems. Plastic prevents the roots from reaching the soil on spreading stems and the underground shoots from surfacing. It also holds high levels of moisture in the soil beneath it. Too much moisture can damage or kill the roots of certain plants.

Inorganic mulches include rock and waste products such as brick chips and synthetic fiber mats. Rock mulches are appropriate for certain ground covers (for example, *Festuca ovina* var. *glauca* and the *Sedum* and *Sempervivum* species), but many other plants have difficulty growing through layers of rock. Rock that contains calcium can raise the soil pH as it weathers. Synthetic fibers and fiber mats are useful for very large ground-cover beds, such as along highways.

Winter Protection

Evergreens (especially broadleaved evergreens) and some other ground-cover plants are susceptible to winter damage, and should be planted in protected sites. Protect plants growing in open, exposed areas with temporary screens or a winter mulch (a loose covering of pine branches, straw, or similar materials that provides insulation for the plants).

A winter mulch shades the foliage of evergreens and helps to hold the soil at a constant temperature, preventing the alternate freezing and thawing that can cause plants to heave out of the soil. Apply a winter mulch after the ground has frozen, and remove it before the plant begins to regrow in the spring.

Plants should be pruned in the spring or in the late fall after they are dormant. Apply fertilizer at the same time. Pruning or fertilizing plants in the late summer can result in new, succulent growth that will not "harden off" before the onset of winter. Evergreens should be watered in the late fall so that they enter the winter with an adequate supply of water.

Watering

Water ground covers thoroughly immediately after planting and continue watering until the plants are established. Water the beds deeply. Shallow watering encourages shallow root growth that is easily damaged during dry periods.

After the plants are established, water them as necessary. Wilting is usually an early signal that plants need watering. Be alert for wilting if your soil is well-drained or during dry periods.

Water ground covers in the morning or early afternoon. If they are watered late in the day, the foliage is likely to remain wet into the evening, when temperatures usually drop. Cool temperatures and wet foliage provide ideal growth conditions for certain diseases.

Newly planted beds can be watered by drip irrigation or by "soaker" hoses laid near the individual plant rows. Be sure to allow adequate time for deep watering. After the beds are covered, use either portable or permanent sprinklers. Water all parts of the bed slowly and uniformly.

Controlling Weeds

Weeds compete with desirable plants for light, moisture, and nutrients. They not only interfere with the establishment of newly planted ground-cover beds but also detract from the appearance of older beds.

Planting large plants or spacing fast-growing plants close together so that they cover quickly will help control weeds. Weeds can also be controlled with mulches, by mechanical means (pulling and hoeing), and (if you have large planting beds) through the use of herbicides.

By blocking the light, mulches inhibit the germination of weed seeds and the growth of seedlings. The weeds that grow through the mulch can be easily removed.

Hoeing is an effective method of controlling weeds in newly planted beds. To prevent the germination of weed seeds, do not break the soil surface except where weeds occur. Be careful not to hoe too deeply or too close to the ground-cover plants — you may damage them. Hoeing is usually not practicable in established beds because of the dense, matted cover. When pulling weeds, remove as much of the root system as possible. Small pieces of roots, especially those of perennial plants, can resprout.

The herbicides used most frequently on ground covers are **preemergents** that control weed seedlings before or as they emerge from the soil. (**Postemergents** are herbicides that are used on weed seedlings after they have emerged from the soil.) Preemergents do not control established weeds. These must be removed by other methods before the herbicide is applied to the planting bed.

Some herbicides remain active in the soil for long periods of time, and may damage newly planted ground covers. Soil fumigants also kill weeds effectively, but are extremely dangerous if used incorrectly because of their high toxicity to humans. Research has established the effectiveness of herbicides mixed into the mulch and postemergence herbicides that kill all grassy weeds in broadleaved ground covers.

Most homeowners do not have large enough ground-cover beds to justify the expense and hazards involved in using herbicides to control weeds. If you decide to apply a herbicide, *follow the directions on the label carefully*. If you hire a professional applicator, be sure that the company he or she represents is reputable and is licensed by the state to apply pesticides. For further information about the proper herbicide for your ground-cover plants and the timing and method of application, consult your county Extension adviser or the horticulture department of your state land-grant university.

After the ground-cover plants have become established, weeds are somewhat easier to control because the shade from the plants reduces the number of germinating weed seeds. It is important to remove the weeds as soon as they appear. Allowing a few weeds to remain in the bed usually results in many more weeds later and a ground-cover stand of reduced quality.

Fertilizing

Most ground covers should be fertilized annually in the spring. A soil test (see page 4) will indicate the type and quantity of fertilizer to be added to the planting bed. For most ground-cover plants, an application of 2 to 4 pounds of 5-10-5 or 5-10-10 fertilizer per 100 square feet of planting bed is satisfactory.

Do not apply granules when the foliage is wet — chemical burn may result. After spreading the fertilizer, wash the granules from the foliage and onto the ground with generous amounts of water. For a quick "greenup," use a soluble fertilizer at the concentration recommended on the package. Root burn can occur if the concentration is higher than recommended, or if the fertilizer is carelessly applied.

Do not fertilize ground covers late in the growing season. Succulent growth will result from late fertilization, and this growth may not "harden off" completely before the onset of cold weather. Soft growth is easily killed by freezing.

Turfgrass fertilizers contain high percentages of nitrogen and small amounts of phosphorus and potassium, and should not be used on most ground covers. Vegetative growth will be promoted at the expense of flowering and fruiting. Do not use "weed and feed" fertilizers. These fertilizers are high in nitrogen and low in phosphorus and potassium, and contain a herbicide that may damage or kill many ground covers.

At planting time, apply a "starter fertilizer" to the backfilled soil when using bare-root plants and other plants that you want to establish quickly. Starter fertilizers have a high percentage of phosphorus, the element necessary for root growth. The breakdown of the mulch and added organic matter also supplies nutrients.

For ground covers that require an acid soil, use a fertilizer (such as an azalea or evergreen fertilizer) that will maintain the acidity of the soil.

Several ground covers require infertile soils for proper growth. These plants should not be planted in rich, fertile soils, and they should not be fertilized unless poor growth or color occurs. High fertility can cause them to become tall, leggy, and unattractive.

Pruning

Ground covers should be pruned to keep the plants in bounds, maintain appearance and vigor, control irregular growth, compensate for root loss when transplanting, and to remove dead, diseased, or damaged plant parts. Always try to maintain the natural appearance of the ground cover.

Ground covers can be divided into several pruning groups. The first group consists of multistemmed, deciduous, shrubby, woody ground covers. These plants can be pruned by the **renewal, rejuvenation** or **heading-back** methods. In renewal pruning, approximately ⅓ of the oldest stems are removed each year to 2 inches above the ground. In rejuvenation pruning, the entire plant is cut to 2 to 4 inches above the ground every 2 or 3 years. Both renewal and rejuvenation pruning "open up" the plant, promote new growth, maintain the size of the plant, and encourage flowering and fruiting. In heading back, individual stems are cut back to a bud or crotch, leaving no stumps. Heading back opens up the center of the plant while maintaining plant size.

Prune deciduous, shrubby ground covers according to when they flower. Those that flower in the spring should be pruned immediately after flowering. Prune summer-flowering, shrubby ground covers in early spring. Do not prune in late summer. The new growth may not "harden off" before the onset of cold weather.

The second pruning group consists of vining or spreading, woody ground covers. To keep these plants in bounds, head back to a crotch or node. Several of these plants (English Ivy and Purpleleaf Wintercreeper, for example) should be sheared each spring to maintain their vigor and denseness. Use hedge shears, a nylon string trimmer, or a rotary mower raised 4 to 6 inches above the ground. Do not mow too close to the ground.

The third group consists of the evergreen junipers. These creeping plants require pruning (preferably in mid-April) to keep them in bounds. Cut back to a crotch in the spring. Evergreen junipers can produce rubbing, crossing branches, and one of the branches should be removed before wounds occur.

The final pruning group consists of the herbaceous ground covers. Many of these plants die to the ground each fall, and the only care required may be the removal of dried litter the following spring so that new growth is unimpeded. After they have flowered, some herbaceous ground covers require shearing, clipping, or mowing to produce a neat, dense growth habit. Do not cut too close to the ground.

The flowering period of certain herbaceous species can be extended by removing the flowers or flower heads as they fade. The faded flowers of some other species should be removed because these plants readily seed themselves, and their seedlings may become a nuisance. Seed production also makes a demand upon the plant's resources, and plant nutrients and products that would otherwise provide better foliage are diverted to producing seeds. The production of fruits is not important for most herbaceous ground covers because the fruits have little ornamental significance.

Propagation

Purchasing ground covers from a nursery or garden center can be expensive. Many ground covers can be easily propagated at home, although a considerable period of time is required to produce usable plants. Many purchased ground-cover plants are at least 2 to 3 years old.

Ground covers may be propagated **sexually** (from seeds) or **asexually.** Many herbaceous and several woody ground covers can be easily produced from seeds. The seedlings are overwintered in a cold frame, and the vigorous species are planted the following spring. The others should be pot-grown through the next 1 or 2 growing seasons, and then planted as container-grown plants in early spring. The offspring produced by sexual propagation may not be identical with the parent plants. Some species and most cultivars and hybrids will not reproduce true to type from seeds.

Asexual propagation is used to produce offspring that are identical with the parent plants. Most cultivars have been selected for a specific characteristic or characteristics. Through asexual propagation, these characteristics, which would probably be lost if the plants were sexually reproduced, are retained. Asexual propagation techniques include **cuttings, layering,** and **division.**

Cuttings are produced when a portion of the parent plant is removed and then treated so that it will continue to grow independently. Many ground covers are propagated by stem cuttings. Sections of stem can be removed in early summer (softwood), mid to late summer (semihardwood), or autumn through winter (hardwood), depending upon the species of woody plant. Certain herbaceous ground covers can also be reproduced by stem cuttings taken during the plant's growing season. Some ground-cover plants can be multiplied by taking a section of root from the parent plant during the winter or early spring. These root cuttings are then treated so that they develop stems, leaves, flowers, and fruits. Several commercial rooting aids are available that will increase the percentage of rooted cuttings if the label directions are followed carefully.

Layering is another form of asexual propagation. The stem sections are treated so that the roots are induced while the stem sections are still attached to the parent plant. As with cuttings, commercial rooting aids will assist rooting.

In division, a part of the parent plant (usually a specialized aboveground or underground stem, fleshy root system, or crown) is divided into several offspring. Spring flowering plants should generally be divided immediately after flowering, summer flowering plants in late summer or early fall, and fall flowering plants in early spring.

Hardiness

The hardiness of a plant (its ability to thrive in a particular environment) is affected by the following: (1) the duration and intensity of sunlight; (2) the length of the growing season; (3) altitude; (4) minimum winter temperatures; (5) the amount and timing of rainfall; (6) the length and severity of summer drouths; (7) soil characteristics and conditions; (8) proximity to a large body of water;

(9) the location of the site with reference to a slope; (10) frost occurrence; (11) humidity; and (12) cultural practices.

The nearer your site approximates the conditions (precipitation, minimum and maximum temperatures, soil characteristics, etc.) under which a plant grew in its native area, the hardier the plant and the better it performs. Even though your landscape is within a particular hardiness zone, various structures and plants may modify the temperature, wind, sun, and precipitation on the actual planting site. The site may also be influenced by the slope of the land, large paved surfaces, low spots, etc.

"Burning" or browning of evergreen foliage during the winter does not necessarily indicate lack of hardiness. The injury, when confined to one side of the plant, may be the result of exposure to winds and winter sun. When the ground is frozen, high winds cause the foliage to lose water rapidly. The plant, unable to replace this water because its roots are encased in frozen soil, suffers dessication (drying out). The air temperature surrounding the plant may suddenly drop as the sun's rays are blocked, causing winter burn. Protection from sun and wind can reduce dessication and winter burn.

The plant hardiness zone map on page 12 has been adapted from the map issued by the U.S. Department of Agriculture. Each of the 10 zones shown on the map represents an area of winter hardiness based upon average minimum winter temperatures ranging from −50° F. or below in Zone 1 to +30° to 40° F. in Zone 10. The temperatures in adjacent zones become increasingly similar near the common boundary. Within each zone many local climates (microclimates) exist that may be warmer or colder than the zone average.

A plant is usually listed in the coldest zone in which it normally grows. The plant can also be expected to live in a warmer zone if growth conditions (rainfall, soil, summer heat, etc.) are comparable or capable of being made comparable through irrigation, soil correction, wind protection, partial shade, or humidity control. Some plants may be grown in isolated areas north of their designated zone, but may not perform well or may suffer from winter injury such as dieback or death of the flower buds.

Nomenclature

The botanical name is the internationally recognized name for a particular plant. Its stem is usually Latin, Greek, or a proper name or descriptive term, and has a Latinized ending. The botanical name consists of two names: the first identifies the **genus,** and the second (**specific epithet**) identifies a particular member of the genus. Together the genus and specific epithet constitute the name of the **species.** The first letter of the genus name is always capitalized, and the specific epithet is commonly written in lower case letters. The species name is underlined or italicized (for example, *Cotoneaster horizontalis*).

The **species** (plural also **species**) is the basic unit in a classification system whose members are structurally similar, have common ancestors, and maintain their characteristic features in nature through innumerable generations.

The **genus** (plural **genera**) may be defined as a more or less closely related and definable group of plants comprising one or more species. The unifying characteristic of a genus is a similarity of flowers. A group of closely related genera is called a **family.** The botanical name of the family is usually recognizable by its —aceae ending. The stem of the name is the name of one of the genera within the family. For example, Cornaceae is the family name in which *Cornus* is a genus.

A **variety** is a subdivision of a species, and exhibits various inheritable morphological characteristics (form and structure) that are perpetuated through both sexual and asexual propagation. A variety is designated by a trinomial (three names). The varietal term is written in lower case and underlined or italicized. It is sometimes written with the abbreviation **var.** placed between the specific epithet and the variety term (for example, *Juniperus chinensis sargentii* or *Juniperus chinensis* var. *sargentii*).

A **cultivar** (the term is a contraction of "cultivated variety") is a group of plants within a particular species that is distinguished by one or more characteristics (morphological, physiological, chemical, etc.), and that, when reproduced sexually or asexually, retains these characteristics. The cultivar term may be one to three names. Each name in the term begins with a capital letter. The term is commonly written inside single quotation marks (as in this book), but it may be preceded by the abbreviation **cv.**, and is not underlined or italicized (for example, *Forsythia viridissima* 'Bronxensis' or *Forsythia viridissima* cv. Bronxensis).

A **clone** (or **clon**) is a group of plants that originated from a single plant, and have been propagated by asexual means (cuttings, grafting, division, budding and layering, etc.) to maintain the exact characteristics of the parent plant.

The name of a hybrid is preceded by a multiplication sign ($\times$) between the generic name and the specific epithet. The names of the parents are listed with the multiplication sign between them. For example, *Symphoricarpos $\times$ chenaultii* is a hybrid of *Symphoricarpos orbiculatus $\times$ Symphoricarpos microphyllus*. In the case of *Symphoricarpos $\times$ chenaultii* 'Hancock', 'Hancock' is a cultivar of the hybrid plant.

Each plant that has been recognized and described has only one valid name — its botanical name (consisting of the name of the genus and the specific epithet). This binomial system of nomenclature was created by Carolus Linnaeus (1707-1778) in his book *Species Plantarum* (1753). The nomenclature is controlled by the International Association for Plant Taxonomy, which issues an *International Code of Botanical Nomenclature* that is strictly adhered to throughout the world. The *International Code of Nomenclature for Cultivated Plants*, which governs the rules for naming cultivars, is issued by the International Union of Botanical Sciences. Both of these Codes are revised periodically.

The botanical name for each of the plants described in this book appears on the upper left of the page, followed by the most often used common name and the hardiness zone or zones in which the plant can be successfully grown. These are followed by the family name and, in some cases, by other common names and the obsolete botanical name or names under which the plant may be listed by certain nurseries or garden centers.

The nomenclature can become confusing in attempting to identify a particular plant. For this reason, you should always use the botanical name when ordering a plant. (It is also helpful to be familiar with the obsolete botanical name or names under which the plant may be listed.) Because common names are not governed by any formal code of nomenclature, and because there are frequently many common names for one species (some of which are obsolete), the use of a common name can lead to mistaken identities.

For information about nurseries and other sources of plants described in this book, consult your county Extension adviser or the horticulture department of your state land-grant university.

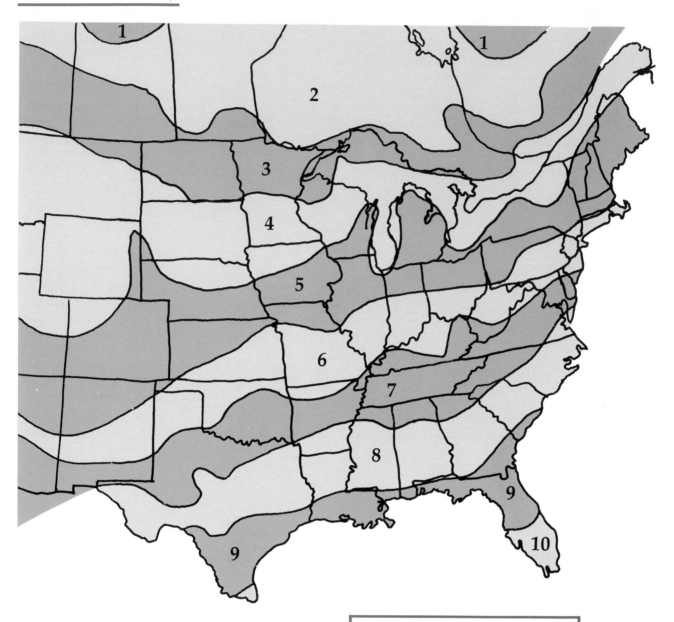

**Range of Average
Annual Minimum Temperatures**

Zone 1   (below −50° F.)
Zone 2   (−50° to −40° F.)
Zone 3   (−40° to −30° F.)
Zone 4   (−30° to −20° F.)
Zone 5   (−20° to −10° F.)
Zone 6   (−10° to 0° F.)
Zone 7   (0° to +10° F.)
Zone 8   (+10° to +20° F.)
Zone 9   (+20° to +30° F.)
Zone 10 (+30° to +40° F.)

Adapted from U.S. Department of Agriculture plant hardiness
zone map of the United States.

Woody
Ground Covers

Typical Entry

Xanthorhiza simplicissima .... botanical name

Yellowroot .... most often used common name

Zone 4 .... hardiness zone

Ranunculaceae (Buttercup family).................. family name

Also known as Shrub Yellowroot .... other common names

May be listed as *Xanthorhiza apiifolia,* .... obsolete botanical names
Zanthorhiza apiifolia

Arctostaphylos uva-ursi

Bearberry

Zone 2

Ericaceae (Heath family)

Also known as Barren Myrtle, Bear's Grape, Billberry, Creashak, Hog Cranberry, Kinnikinick, Mealberry, Mountain Box, Red Bearberry, Sandberry

May be listed as *Arctostaphylos officinalis, Arbutus uva-ursi, Uva-ursi procumbens*

For a color illustration of *Arctostaphylos uva-ursi,* see page 57.

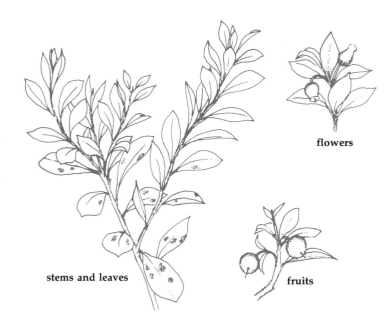

flowers

stems and leaves

fruits

Bearberry is a creeping, mat-forming, evergreen ground cover that grows ½ to 1 foot high and 2 to 5 feet wide. The branches root as they spread and turn up at their ends. Growth rate is slow while the plants are becoming established, but becomes more rapid later. Texture is fine in both summer and winter.

Leaves. The leaves are alternate, simple, and ½ to 1¼ inches long, with a leafstalk ¼ inch long or less. The leaf is longer than it is wide, with a rounded apex and a wedge-shaped base. The margins roll downward, and are sometimes hairy fringed. The leaves are glossy dark green above and lighter green beneath, turning a reddish bronze in the fall and winter. They are leathery and hairless except when young.

Stems. The young stems are glabrous (without hairs) or minutely hairy; the older stems are reddish to grayish, with papery, exfoliating bark.

Flowers. The urn-shaped, white to pinkish flowers are borne in terminal clusters from April through June. The ¼-inch-long flowers are perfect (with both stamens and pistils), 4- to 5-lobed, and have stalks about ⅛ inch long.

Fruits. The fruits are lustrous, nearly globe-shaped, berrylike red drupes (stone fruits) about ¼ to ⅓ inch long. They are dry, mealy, have 4 to 10 nutlets, and serve as food for wildlife. The fruits are borne from July through September, and usually persist until March.

Culture. This plant grows best in poor, well-drained, acid soil. A pH of less than 5.5 will keep the planting dense and vigorous. Bearberry is salt tolerant. It grows well in full sun to light shade, and tolerates strong winds.

Bearberry is difficult to transplant. Container-grown plants or squares of sod can be used. Space single container-grown plants 1 to 2 feet apart. Plant in early spring. If you use sod for transplanting, lay the sod in place and sift sand between the squares. Shear the sod to 6 inches after laying it. Keep both the sod or container-grown plants well watered. Mulching will aid in establishment.

After Bearberry is established, it requires little care. Pruning is needed only to keep the plant within bounds. Thicken by shearing or by using a rotary mower (set to 6 inches high) immediately after flowering. Occasionally apply an acid fertilizer.

Propagation is by seeds, division, layering, and cuttings taken in late summer and early spring.

This plant is generally pest-free, although black mildew, leaf galls, and rusts have been reported.

Uses. Bearberry can be used on protected slopes or on level ground, and is especially attractive beneath other broad-leaved evergreens. It is often used on highway slopes to control erosion. Because Bearberry has a tendency to open in the center, it may not be suitable for certain large areas.

Arctostaphylos uva-ursi is native to North America, Europe, and Asia. It has been in cultivation since 1800.

Comptonia peregrina

Sweetfern

Zone 2

Myricaceae (Sweet Gale family)

May be listed as *Comptonia asplenifolia, Myrica asplenifolia*

For a color illustration of *Comptonia peregrina*, see page 57.

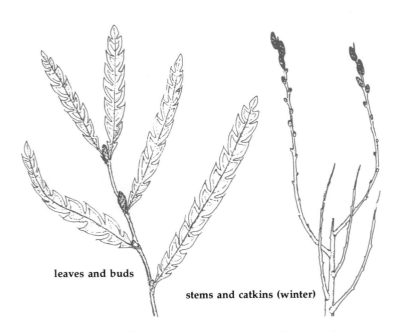

leaves and buds

stems and catkins (winter)

Sweetfern is a broad-rounded to flat-topped, thicket-forming, deciduous ground cover that grows 2 to 4 feet high and spreads by underground stems 4 to 8 feet wide. Texture is medium-fine in leaf and medium after the leaves have dropped. Growth rate is medium.

Leaves. The alternate, simple leaves emerge light green, becoming a lustrous dark green by midsummer. They are pubescent (sometimes with resinous dots) and 2 to 6 inches long and ½ to ¾ inch wide, with a leafstalk. The leaf margins have 6 to 20 broad, rounded to bristle-tipped lobes that continue almost to the midrib. Fall color is not ornamental.

Stems. The young stems are yellowish, greenish, or reddish brown, and are pubescent or have resinous dots; the older stems are yellowish to coppery brown. The crushed stems and leaves are aromatic.

Flowers. The male and female flowers are distinct but usually occur on the same plant. Male flowers (staminate) are borne at the end of the stems, and are cylindrical catkins up to ⅗ inch long. The female flowers (pistillate) are ½ to 1 inch in diameter, and are in rounded clusters. The flowers are yellow-green to brownish, and appear from April through May (usually before the leaves emerge).

Fruits. The fruits are egg-shaped, burrlike, olive-brown nutlets from ⅕ to ⅜ inch long. They are borne in clusters from August through October, and are eaten by birds.

Culture. Sweetfern grows best in full sun in well-drained, dry, acid (pH of 5.5 to 6.5) soil.

This plant tolerates poor, sterile soil, salt, drouth, and partial shade. It grows on both dry, gravelly sites and moist, organic ones.

Sweetfern can be transplanted from sod or container-grown plants. Container-grown plants are easier to transplant than sod because Sweetfern has a stringy root system. Space plants 1½ to 2 feet apart. If you transplant from sod, use large pieces of sod and prune the plants to the ground. Mulching aids in establishment. After Sweetfern is established, it needs little care. It has the ability to fix nitrogen, and fertilizer is rarely necessary. Because the plants form thickets by suckering, pruning is required only to keep the plants within bounds.

Propagation is by seeds, division, layering, stem cuttings of juvenile wood, and root cuttings. Root cuttings should be 1/16 to ½ inch in diameter and 2 to 5 inches long (the smaller the diameter, the longer the cutting). Take root cuttings in late winter to early spring. Place ½ inch deep in individual pots, with sand and peat as the potting medium.

Sweetfern is not seriously affected by insect pests or diseases. It is, however, an alternate host for a rust disease that can affect some pines.

Uses. Sweetfern can be used on level ground and on slopes as an erosion control. It is especially effective in naturalized areas.

Comptonia peregrina is native from Nova Scotia to North Carolina, and west to Michigan and Indiana. It was introduced in 1714.

Comptonia peregrina var. *asplenifolia* has smaller leaves and catkins than the species, and is less pubescent.

16

Cornus canadensis

Bunchberry

Zone 2

Cornaceae (Dogwood family)

Also known as Bunchberry Dogwood, Crackerberry, Creeping Dogwood, Dwarf Cornel, Puddingberry

May be listed as *Chamaepericlymenum canadense*

For a color illustration of *Cornus canadensis*, see page 57.

stems, leaves, and flowers

Bunchberry is a delicate, highly ornamental, prostrate, deciduous ground cover that grows 5 to 12 inches high and spreads to 2 feet wide. As the roots spread, new stems arise to form wide colonies. Growth rate is slow. Texture is medium-fine.

Leaves. The leaves are simple, whorled in groups of 4 to 6, and 1 to 3 inches long, without a leafstalk. They are borne on a single stem, and held horizontally. Smaller leaves appear oppositely near the base of the stalk. The leaf is oval to egg-shaped, pointed at both ends, and is hairless or slightly hairy. There are 5 to 7 parallel veins in each leaf blade. The margin is entire. The leaves vary in color from dull to glossy dark green, turning yellow to wine red in the fall.

Flowers. The small, fertile, greenish yellow flowers are densely clustered at the end of the long flower stalk, and are not ornamental. They are surrounded by 4 to 6 showy white bracts that are oval-shaped and ⅓ to 1 inch long. The flowers are borne from May through June, and resemble the flowers of *Cornus florida* (Flowering Dogwood).

Fruits. The fruits are berrylike red drupes (stone fruits) that are ¼ inch in diameter and are clustered at the end of the fruit stalk. They ripen in August, and persist on the plant until October or until they are eaten by birds.

Culture. Bunchberry is native to woodlands, and requires a cool, moist, well-drained, acidic soil. The soil should contain large amounts of organic matter, and have a pH of about 4.5.

This plant grows well in full sun in the spring, but requires a cool, moist, shady to semishady location during the summer. Because the plants must be protected from the summer sun, they should be grown beneath deciduous trees or in the full shade of evergreen trees or shrubs.

Bunchberry is a delicate plant that requires special care. It can be transplanted from sod or container-grown plants. Space plants 6 inches apart. Moisture is essential until the plants are established. An acid mulch is also helpful. Bunchberry is not invasive, and is easily kept within bounds.

Propagation is by seeds, layering, and division in the spring.

This plant is not seriously affected by insect pests or diseases.

Uses. Because of its outstanding beauty throughout several seasons, Bunchberry should be used in highly visible locations. It grows well in naturalized areas beneath broad-leaved evergreens and other acid-loving plants.

Cornus canadensis is native from Labrador to Alaska, south to West Virginia, and in New Mexico, Colorado, California, and eastern Asia. It was introduced in 1758.

Cornus sericea 'Kelseyi'

Kelsey Red-Osier Dogwood

Zone 4

Cornaceae (Dogwood family)

May also be listed as *Cornus stolonifera* 'Kelseyi'

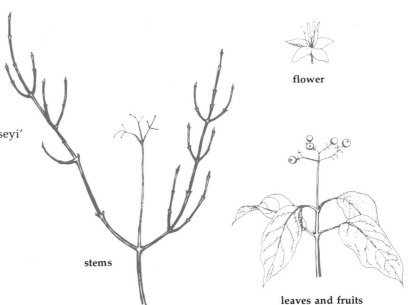

flower

stems

leaves and fruits

Kelsey Red-Osier Dogwood is a dense, low-growing, rounded, deciduous, shrublike ground cover that grows 1½ to 2½ feet high and spreads to 2 feet wide. It is much-branched and clump-forming. Growth rate is medium. Texture is coarse.

Leaves. The leaves are opposite, simple, and stalked. The leaf is oval, with a pointed apex and a rounded base. The margin is entire. The upper leaf surface is bright green, and the lower surface is pale green. The autumn color is ineffective in certain areas and brown to purple-maroon in others.

Stems. Some young stems are bright red. As the stems mature, they become brownish red to brown. The pith is white.

Flowers. The offwhite flowers are borne in 1½- to 2-inch, flattopped clusters from late May through early June. They do not commonly occur, and are not showy.

Fruits. The fruits are globe-shaped, berrylike, white drupes (stone fruits) that are seldom borne.

Culture. Kelsey Red-Osier Dogwood grows best in moist sites. It will, however, tolerate most soils, including dry, gravelly, or sandy soils.

Full sun to partial shade is the recommended exposure.

Transplanting is not difficult. Container-grown plants can be transplanted at any season provided that adequate moisture is available during dry periods. Space plants 1 to 1½ feet apart. After the plants are established, they require little care except for occasional pruning.

Pruning older stems in the spring before new growth starts will keep the plant developing new stems that are the brightest in color. Multi-stemmed plants can tolerate fairly severe shearing to the near ground level in the spring (see "rejuvenation pruning," page 9).

Propagation is by layering and by both softwood and hardwood cuttings.

Several foliar diseases can occur in areas with extremely poor soil drainage, inadequate air circulation, or high humidity. Treatment may be necessary for leaf blight and leaf spot diseases (ask your county Extension adviser for recommendations). Twig blights and root rots have also been reported. Scale and other insect pests can seriously damage these plants.

Uses. Kelsey Red-Osier Dogwood can be used to cover both large and small areas. Because of its coarse texture, this plant may not be suitable for refined gardens.

Cornus mas 'Nana' (Dwarf Corneliancherry Dogwood) is another dwarf dogwood cultivar with a growth habit similar to that of *Cornus sericea* 'Kelseyi'. This plant is an upright, spherical bush that is stiffer, cleaner, and slower growing than Kelsey Red-Osier Dogwood, and is not as satisfactory as a ground cover.

Cotoneaster adpressus

Creeping Cotoneaster

Zone 4

Rosaceae (Rose family)

May be listed as *Cotoneaster horizontalis* var. *adpressa*

stems, leaves, and fruits

Creeping Cotoneaster is a prostrate, matlike, irregularly branched, dense, mounding, deciduous ground cover that grows 1 to 2 feet high and spreads 4 to 6 feet wide. The spreading branches root wherever they touch soil, and may "pile on" themselves. Growth rate is slow. Texture is fine.

Leaves. The dull, dark-green leaves are alternate, simple, and ¼ to ⅝ inch long, with a very short leafstalk. The leaf is broadly oval to almost rounded. The apex can be blunt to somewhat pointed, and is bristle-tipped. The margin is entire and slightly wavy. The under surfaces of young leaves may be slightly hairy. The leaves may turn reddish in the autumn.

Stems. The stems are stiff and slightly hairy.

Flowers. The inconspicuous pinkish flowers are ¼ to ⅜ inch in diameter, and are very shortly stalked. The petals are borne upright, and the flowers occur either singly or in pairs from May through June.

Two cultivars of *Cotoneaster adpressus* are of interest: *Cotoneaster adpressus* var. *praecox* (may be listed as *Cotoneaster praecox*) and *Cotoneaster adpressus* 'Little Gem'. *Cotoneaster adpressus* var. *praecox* (Early Cotoneaster) is more vigorous than the species, and will grow to 2 feet in height. The leaves and fruits are somewhat larger than those of Creeping Cotoneaster, and the flowers are pink-tinged purplish. *Cotoneaster adpressus* 'Little Gem' is a very small plant (a 10-year-old plant was only 6 inches high and 12 to 15 inches wide), and apparently does not produce flowers or fruits.

Fruits. The fruits are nearly globose, bright red, berrylike pomes that are about ¼ inch long and usually contain 2 nutlets. The fruits are borne from August through September.

Culture. See *Cotoneaster horizontalis*, page 21.
Uses. See *Cotoneaster horizontalis*, page 21.

Cotoneaster adpressus was introduced from western China about 1896.

stems

19

Cotoneaster dammeri

Bearberry Cotoneaster
Zone 5

Rosaceae (Rose family)

May be listed as *Cotoneaster humifusa*

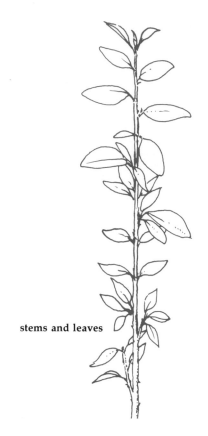

stems and leaves

Bearberry Cotoneaster is a low-growing, prostrate, matlike, deciduous to evergreen ground cover that grows up to 1 foot high and spreads 6 to 10 feet wide. The spreading branches root wherever they touch soil. Growth rate is fast. Texture is fine.

Leaves. The leaves are evergreen in mild climates and semievergreen in colder areas. If grown in a cool, exposed site, the plant may be deciduous.

The leaves are alternate, simple, and ¾ to 1¼ inches long, with a short leafstalk. The leaf is usually narrowly oval. The apex is rounded, pointed, or (rarely) notched, and often has a bristle tip. The base is wedge-shaped. The margin is entire. The upper leaf surface is glossy dark green and hairless; the underside is paler green, and may be sparsely hairy with a netlike venation when the leaf is young. The leaves may take on a purple tinge in late fall or early winter.

Stems. The young stems are hairy; the older stems become hairless and reddish brown.

Flowers. The white flowers are short stalked and about ⅜ inch wide. They are usually borne singly from May through June, and are often sparsely produced.

Fruits. The scarlet pomes are about ¼ inch wide, and are borne in late summer. They are almost globe-shaped, and usually contain 5 nutlets.

Culture. See *Cotoneaster horizontalis*, page 21.

Uses. See *Cotoneaster horizontalis*, page 21.

Cotoneaster dammeri is native to central China, and was introduced in 1900.

A popular cultivar is *Cotoneaster dammeri* 'Skogsholmen' (Skogsholm Bearberry Cotoneaster). This plant is more vigorous than the species, and has a mounded habit with somewhat arching branches. It will grow to over 2 feet high, and may spread to more than 6 feet wide. The leaves sometimes turn reddish orange in the autumn, and the plant may put out new growth that can be killed during the winter. Skogsholm Bearberry Cotoneaster does not fruit freely.

Cotoneaster dammeri 'Coral Beauty' (may be listed as *Cotoneaster dammeri* 'Royal Beauty' and 'Pink Beauty') is a cultivar that freely produces coral-colored fruits.

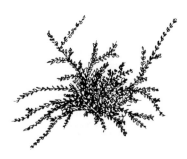

Cotoneaster horizontalis

Rockspray Cotoneaster

Zone 4

Rosaceae (Rose family)

Also known as Fishbone Cotoneaster, Herringbone Cotoneaster, Plumed Cotoneaster, Quinceberry, Rock Cotoneaster

May be listed as *Cotoneaster davidiana*

For color illustrations of *Cotoneaster horizontalis*, see page 57.

stems and fruits (winter)

leaves and flowers

Rockspray Cotoneaster is a dense, deciduous to semievergreen ground cover that grows 3 to 5 feet high and spreads 8 to 10 feet wide. The branches spread horizontally, and can recurve or arch. Growth rate is medium. Texture is fine when the plant is in leaf, and medium after the leaves have dropped.

Leaves. The dark-green leaves are ⅕ to ½ inch long, alternate, simple, and have a short, hairy leafstalk. They are broadly oval to nearly rounded, with a pointed, bristle tip and a wedge-shaped base. The margin is entire and flat. The leaf surface is shining and hairless above and slightly hairy beneath. In cooler regions, the leaves turn reddish-purple in the fall.

Stems. The stiff, hairy branches grow in flat fans, with branchlets arising alternately along the stem in a fishbone pattern.

Flowers. The perfect, inconspicuous, pinkish flowers are ¼ inch in diameter. They are borne profusely (singly or in pairs) from May through June.

Fruits. The glossy, berrylike, red pomes are ⅕ to ¼ inch in diameter, globe-shaped to oval, and usually have 3 nutlets. They are borne in early fall and persist into winter.

Culture. Cotoneasters grow best in a well-drained, neutral to slightly acidic soil. They tolerate a great variety of soil types (alkaline or acid, rich or poor, hot or dry), but do not grow well in heavy or wet soils.

For best flower and fruit production, cotoneasters should be grown in full sun. These plants can tolerate light shade and windy sites but not heavy shade. They also should not be planted beneath deciduous trees because fallen leaves can damage the prostrate growing stems.

Cotoneasters are best transplanted from small, container-grown plants because they have sparse root systems. Do not use bare-root plants. Large plants transplant with difficulty. Plant in the spring, and space plants 1 to 4 feet apart. These plants appear to their best advantage if planted in areas that do not restrict their growth. Occasional pruning may be necessary, but the plants become unattractive when constantly pruned. Deciduous plants should be pruned in late winter or early spring, and evergreen plants should be pruned immediately before growth starts. "Heading back" (see page 9) is usually the only pruning required.

Because of their low growth and twiggy habit, some cotoneasters can collect litter, and accumulated trash should be removed. Although the branches of certain cotoneasters spread, the branches are not dense, and weeds can grow between them.

Propagation is by seeds, division, layering, and soft-, semihard-, and hardwood cuttings.

Cotoneasters can be affected by leaf spots, cankers, fire blight, hawthorn lace bug, scales, cotoneaster webworm, sinuate pear borer, pear leaf blister mite, and red spider. Lace bug, mites, and fire blight can be serious.

Uses. These plants can be used on level ground or as soil binders on slopes. Large cotoneasters should be planted in areas where they have space to spread. They adapt well to rock gardens, and are attractive cascading over boulders.

Cotoneaster horizontalis was introduced about 1880 from western China.

Cytisus decumbens

Prostrate Broom

Zone 6

Fabaceae (Pea family)

May be listed as *Genista decumbens, Genista prostrata, Spartium decumbens*

For a color illustration of *Cytisus decumbens,* see page 58.

stem, leaves, and pod

stem and flowers

Prostrate Broom is a dense, mat-forming, prostrate, deciduous ground cover that grows to 8 inches high. The branches spread in all directions, and can root wherever they touch soil. They may "mound up" as they grow. Because the branches remain green all winter, the plant provides winter color. Growth rate is slow. Texture is fine.

Leaves. The leaves are alternate, simple, and ¼ to ¾ inch long and ¹⁄₁₆ to ¹⁄₁₈ inch wide, without a leafstalk. The leaves are narrowly oval-shaped and pubescent on both surfaces, with the undersides being hairier. They are soft green, and there is no ornamental fall color.

Stems. The green branchlets are 5-angled, and may be pubescent.

Flowers. The bright yellow, pealike flowers are borne in axillary clusters in joints of the previous year's growth. Clusters of 1 to 3 flowers are produced from May through June, with sporadic production until August. The flowers are ½ to ⅝ inch long, and have hairy sepals.

Fruits. The hairy, 1-inch pods contain 3 to 4 seeds, and are not ornamental.

Culture. Prostate Broom grows best in soil that is dry, well-drained, slightly acidic, and not too rich. It also grows well in sandy soil and tolerates drouth. With proper drainage, this plant can be grown in areas with heavy rainfall provided that the soil surface dries quickly.

Prostrate Broom grows best in full sun, and should not be planted in shady areas. It tolerates salty air and windy conditions.

Large plants of Prostrate Broom are difficult to transplant. Small container-grown plants

transplant best, and should be place directly into their permanent location 12 inches apart. Because Prostrate Broom has the ability to fix nitrogen, fertilizer is rarely needed. Stem dieback may occur during severe winters, and the damaged stems should be pruned after flowering. Do not cultivate beneath the plants after they are established.

Propagation is by seeds, layering, and soft-wood or hardwood cuttings.

This plant is not seriously affected by insect pests or diseases.

Uses. Prostrate Broom can be used on slopes or level ground. It grows well in rock gardens.

Cytisus decumbens is native to southern Europe, and was introduced in 1775.

Cytisus procumbens (Ground Broom) is a closely related species. It is quite similar to Prostrate Broom except that the leaves are 1¼ inches long, the plant grows to 30 inches high, and the undersides of the leaves and the flower stalks are more pubescent. Ground Broom will spread and form a mat several feet wide.

Euonymus fortunei selections

Wintercreepers

Celastraceae (Staff-tree family)

For a color illustration of *Euonymus fortunei* 'Colorata', see page 58.

The wintercreepers are a group of semievergreen to evergreen plants ranging from trailing to climbing to shrubby forms. The trailing forms usually root wherever their stems touch the soil. Some of the shrubby, trailing forms can climb by means of aerial rootlets to more than 20 feet.

The variability of this group is the result of its ability to sport (mutate or change). Several different forms can occur on a single plant. These plants also vary in leaf types and in the ability to flower and fruit. Usually the shrubby forms are most likely to produce flowers and fruits. Leaves vary in length from ½ inch to over 2 inches. Leaf coloration ranges from bright green to dark green, and can be variegated with white, yellow, and pink. Several selections have leaves that turn purplish in the autumn.

Leaves. The semievergreen to evergreen leaves are opposite, simple, and are usually toothed, thick, and leathery.

Flowers. The flowering forms produce flowers in several clusters in the leaf axils. The greenish white to whitish flowers are perfect, and are borne from June through July. They are stalked and are not showy.

Fruits. The nearly globe-shaped fruits are about ⅓ inch in diameter, and are borne from October through November, often persisting into winter. The outer capsule may vary in color from scarlet to pink to white, and opens to expose a fleshy, orangish seed coat.

Culture. *Euonymus fortunei* selections grow best in a moist, well-drained, fertile soil, although they will grow in a wide variety of soils. These plants are pH adaptable, and can tolerate drouth except in extremely dry areas. They are not suitable for boggy or wet areas, but can provide some erosion control when grown on slopes.

Wintercreeper selections will tolerate full sun to quite heavy shade. Although they tolerate summer wind, protection from winter wind and sun is necessary to reduce drying and burn. They may grow more slowly in the shade.

Transplanting wintercreeper selections is not difficult. They should be planted in the spring, and plants should be spaced ½ to 2 feet apart, depending upon the selection. The growth rate usually increases once the plants are established. Wintercreepers should be pruned in early spring; several of the trailing forms should also be sheared at this time. A rotary mower raised to its maximum height works well. Fertilizer should also be applied in the spring if the leaves begin to lose their healthy green color. A complete, balanced fertilizer is recommended.

Propagation is by layering, division in the spring or fall, and stem cuttings taken from June through September.

These plants are susceptible to several insect pests and diseases. Anthracnose, crown gall, leaf spots, powdery mildews, aphids, thrips, and scales have been reported. The scales are particularly troublesome in hot, dry areas. Ask your county Extension adviser for recommendations.

Uses. Wintercreeper selections can be used in large or small areas, and on level or sloping ground. The small-leaved forms are effective in small, refined areas, and climbers can be used to hide unsightly views. Selecting the proper plant for a particular area is the key to success and satisfaction.

Euonymus fortunei is native to central and western China.

Because *Euonymus fortunei* mutates so readily, many selections are available. The selections described on pages 24-26 have been used successfully as ground covers in the Midwest.

23

Euonymus fortunei 'Colorata'

Purpleleaf Wintercreeper

Zone 4

May be listed as *Euonymus coloratus, Euonymus fortunei* var. *colorata, Euonymus radicans* forma *colorata*

stem and leaves

Purpleleaf Wintercreeper is a dense, vigorous, trailing, semievergreen to evergreen ground cover that grows ½ to 1½ feet high and spreads widely. The stems creep along the ground and root wherever they touch soil. The end of the branches ascend, and the plant can climb to over 20 feet high by means of aerial rootlets. This plant is mildly invasive. Growth rate is fast. Texture is medium-fine. As a ground cover, Purpleleaf Wintercreeper apparently does not produce flowers or fruits.

The leaves are 1 to 2 inches long, without prominent venation. During the summer, the leaves are a deep, glossy green. As the autumn weather cools, they turn a dark red-purple on the upper sides and lighter on the undersides. If Purpleleaf Wintercreeper is grown in an unprotected area, the leaves may drop. In protected areas, the leaves will resume their green color as the weather warms in the spring. The plant seems to color best when grown in poor soil.

Purpleleaf Wintercreeper is often listed as a botanic variety (*Euonymus fortunei* var. *colorata*). Variations in the intensity of winter coloring may be the result of different clonal sources. If the plant is a cultivar, variations in color may be the result of environmental differences.

This plant grows well in most landscape areas, and can be used on slopes. It should be mowed to 4 to 8 inches high in the spring to keep it dense and vigorous. Scales can be a severe problem.

Euonymus fortunei 'Colorata' was introduced in 1914.

Euonymus fortunei var. *radicans*

Common Wintercreeper

Zone 4

May be listed as *Euonymus japonica* var. *radicans, Euonymus japonica* var. *viridis, Euonymus radicans*

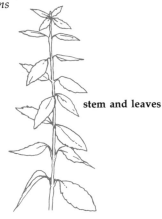

stem and leaves

Common Wintercreeper is a variable, semievergreen to evergreen ground cover that can trail, climb, or become rather shrubby. As a trailer, it is low-growing, somewhat mounded, and wide-spreading. It roots as it spreads. If supported, Common Wintercreeper can climb more than 20 feet high by means of aerial rootlets. As the plant matures, it becomes erect and bushy. It may flower and fruit at this stage. Texture is medium. Growth rate is fairly fast.

The uniform semievergreen to evergreen leaves are ½ to 1¼ inches long and ¼ to ⅝ inch wide, with a short leafstalk. The leaf is narrowly oval, with a blunt to pointed apex and a tapered to rounded base. The margins are toothed. The leaves are dark green and hairless, leathery, thick, and usually not glossy.

Common Wintercreeper should be protected from winter sun and wind that can dry and burn it. It competes well with weeds, but it is susceptible to crown gall and occasionally scales.

Euonymus fortunei var. *radicans* is native to Japan and southern Korea. It was introduced about 1865.

Euonymus fortunei var. *vegeta*

Bigleaf Wintercreeper

Zone 4

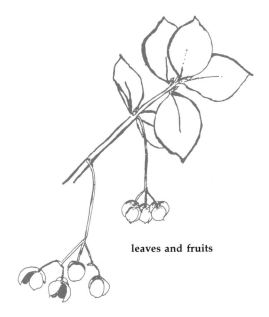

leaves and fruits

Bigleaf Wintercreeper is a low, spreading, mounded, shrubby, evergreen ground cover that grows 2 to 5 feet high and spreads to 4 feet wide. This plant has both prostrate and erect stems, and, if supported, can climb by means of aerial rootlets. Growth rate is medium to fast. Texture is medium-fine.

The semievergreen leaves are 1 to 1½ inches long and broadly oval to almost circular. The apex is broadly pointed to nearly blunt. The margins have rounded teeth, and the texture is leathery. The leaves are deep green.

The greenish white flowers are borne in large, dense axillary clusters from June through July. They are not ornamental.

The large, showy fruit capsules are greenish white to pinkish outside. They open to expose an orange, berrylike, fleshy seed coat that is ⅓ inch in diameter. This plant seems to produce the most abundant and largest fruits of the *Euonymus fortunei* selections. Birds may eat the fruits.

Bigleaf Wintercreeper can be used as a low ground cover if it is sheared when it is young and thereafter. Shear in the spring. This plant needs protection from winter wind and sun, and grows best in partial shade. It should be grown in well-drained soil.

Scales and crown gall can be especially troublesome on Bigleaf Wintercreeper.

Euonymus fortunei var. *vegeta* is native to Japan. It was introduced in 1876.

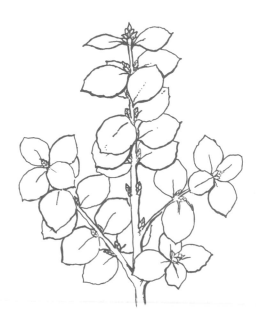

stems and leaves

Small-leaved selections of *Euonymus fortunei*

Zone 5

stem and leaves

The small-leaved selections of *Euonymus fortunei* should be grown in protected areas. They should not be allowed to dry out, and an application of a complete, balanced fertilizer in the spring is recommended. These plants may not cover densely enough to prevent weeds from becoming a problem. The evergreen selections described below are similar, and may be sold interchangeably.

Euonymus fortunei var. *acuta* is the fastest growing plant of the group. The deep-green leaves may turn bronze in the winter. The plant hugs the ground.

'Kewensis' (Kew Wintercreeper) is delicate and slow growing. The leaves are the smallest of the group (usually ¼ to ½ inch long). The plant may climb if support is available, but it usually grows only 2 inches from the ground.

'Longwood' (Longwood Wintercreeper) is slow growing, and may reach 4 to 6 inches in height. It has slightly larger leaves than the Kew Wintercreeper, and seems to be somewhat hardier.

'Minima' (Baby Wintercreeper) is prostrate, sterile, and does not climb readily. The leaves are ⅝ inch long, with distinct, light-colored veins on the upper surface.

Variegated-leaf selections of *Euonymus fortunei*

Zone 5

For a color illustration of *Euonymus fortunei* 'Silver Queen', see page 58.

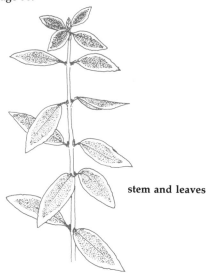

stem and leaves

The variegated evergreen selections described below will be whiter if they are grown in the shade rather than in full sun. Most of these plants assume a purplish cast in the winter. In general, they are less hardy than the solid, green-leaved forms.

'Emerald Gaiety' is erect, 4 to 5 feet high, and has white leaf margins.

'Emerald and Gold' is a tight-branching shrub with yellow, variegated leaves. It grows up to 4 feet high.

'Gracilis' ('Roseo-marginata', 'Argenteo-marginata') is a variable form that can climb. The leaves are usually less than 1½ inches long, and are variously margined with white, yellow, or pink. They are mostly pink in winter.

'Silver Queen' is shrubby and slow growing, reaching 2 feet in height and spreading to 2 feet wide. It may climb to 9 feet high with support. The leaves have creamy, yellow margins when they unfold and white margins at maturity. 'Silver Queen' bears flowers and fruits, and may be a sport of a solid, green-leaved, shrubby form, 'Carrierei'.

'Variegata' is usually a trailing and climbing form that grows 15 to 24 inches high. It may be a sport of *Euonymus fortunei* var. *radicans*. The leaves are gray-green with white margins. If the plant becomes shrubby, it may bear flowers and fruits. Some authorities believe that 'Gracilis' and 'Variegata' are the same plant.

Forsythia viridissima 'Bronxensis'

Bronx Greenstem Forsythia

Zone 5

Oleaceae (Olive family)

For color illustrations of *Forsythia viridissima* 'Bronxensis', see page 58.

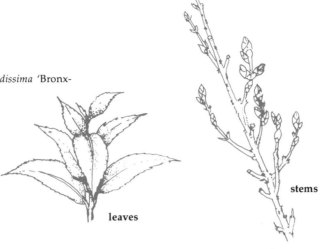

leaves

stems

flowers

Bronx Greenstem Forsythia is a low, twiggy, mounded, deciduous, shrublike ground cover that grows 1 to 2 feet high and spreads 2 to 4 feet wide. Texture and growth rate are medium.

Leaves. The leaves are opposite, simple, from ¾ to 1¾ inches long, and stalked. The leaf is about ½ inch wide, and is somewhat diamond-shaped, with a long, tapering apex and a wedge-shaped base. The margins are toothed above the base. Summer color is bright green above and a paler green beneath. Fall color is an ineffective green-yellow in good soil; in poor soil, the leaves may turn purplish bronze.

Stems. The stems are greenish when young, becoming light greenish brown and covered with lenticels (small, corky spots) as the plant matures. The pith is chambered throughout.

Flowers. The small, bright yellow, 4-lobed flowers are borne profusely in April before the leaves appear. They are borne along the stems on old wood. During extreme winters, the flower buds can be killed, especially those not covered by snow. The plants often need to be established for 2 to 3 years before flowering begins.

Fruits. The fruits are hard capsules that are not ornamental.

Culture. Bronx Greenstem Forsythia grows well in most good soils with a pH of 4.5 to 7.5. It flowers best in full sun, but will grow in partial shade. After the plant is established, it tolerates drouth and city conditions.

Container-grown plants can be transplanted during any season provided that moisture is available during dry periods. Space plants 1 to 2 feet apart. After the plants are established, little care is necessary. Prune immediately after

flowering. To promote greater density, shear multi-stemmed plants close to the ground.

Propagation is by layering and by softwood, semihardwood, and hardwood cuttings. These cuttings root easier than previously reported.

This plant is not seriously affected by insect pests or diseases.

Uses. Bronx Greenstem Forsythia can be used effectively on level ground or slopes in both large and small areas. Its winter appearance may be objectionable in highly visible sites.

Forsythia viridissima 'Bronxensis' occurred as a seedling from *Forsythia viridissima* var. *koreana* in 1928. It was named in 1947 by the curator of the New York Botanic Gardens in the Bronx.

Forsythia 'Arnold Dwarf' (Arnold Dwarf Forsythia) is a related plant resulting from a cross between *Forsythia* × *intermedia* and *Forsythia japonica*. It grows up to 3 feet high and spreads 6 to 8 feet wide, with a mounded habit and low, arching branches that root wherever they touch moist soil. For this reason, Arnold Dwarf Forsythia is effective on slopes and banks. The plant may not flower until it has been established from 6 to 8 years. The flowers are small, greenish yellow, and sparsely produced. Arnold Dwarf Forsythia is less attractive than *Forsythia viridissima* 'Bronxensis'. It was introduced by the Arnold Arboretum, Jamaica Plain, Massachusetts, in 1941.

Hedera helix

English Ivy

Zone 5

Araliaceae (Ginseng family)

For a color illustration of *Hedera helix,* see page 59.

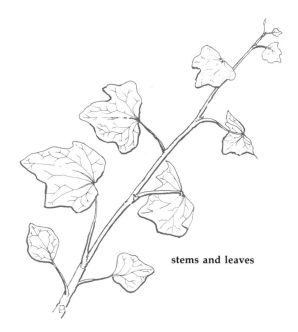

stems and leaves

English Ivy is a low-growing, trailing ever-green ground cover that grows 6 to 10 inches high and spreads widely. As it spreads, it roots at the nodes. This plant also has the ability to climb; if supported, it can climb to 100 feet high by means of aerial rootlets. Growth rate is fast. Texture is medium.

English Ivy has both a juvenile and a mature growth stage. In the juvenile or sterile stage, it is a trailing, wide-spreading ground cover or a climber, the stems are flexible, and the plant does not flower or fruit. The mature or fertile stage occurs when a climber reaches about 15 feet on a support or climbs to the top of its support. Both flowers and fruits are produced, the stems become stiff, and the habit is bushy. In this stage, English Ivy does not climb, and can be propagated and used as a broad-leaved ever-green shrub.

Leaves. In the juvenile stage, the leaves are alternate, simple, and ½ to 5 inches long, with a leafstalk. They have 3 to 5 variable lobes, and are egg-shaped, with the broadest part near the heart-shaped or straight-across base. The margins are nearly entire, and the leaves can be thick and leathery. The upper leaf surface is usually glossy dark green, with whitish venation; the underside is pale or yellowish green.

The mature leaves are oval to narrowly oval and unlobed, with a straight-across to wedge-shaped base. These leaves are usually a paler green than the leaves in the juvenile stage.

Flowers. The pale-green, perfect flowers are borne only on mature plants. They occur in small, round clusters from September through October, and are not showy.

Fruits. The black to dark-purplish, berrylike fruits are ¼ inch in diameter. They occur only on mature plants from April through May following flowering, and may be poisonous.

Culture. English Ivy grows best in rich, well-drained, moist, acid soil with large amounts of organic matter, although it tolerates a wide variety of soils. It will also tolerate dry sites after it has become established. The plants are shallow rooted, but grow well on slight slopes.

In the Midwest, English Ivy grows best in the shade and requires protection from winter sun and wind that can cause dryness and burn. In other areas of the United States, it will grow in full sun to heavy shade.

English Ivy is easily transplanted from container-grown plants in the spring. Space plants 12 inches apart, and trim the stems to 6 inches high at planting time. Growth may be slow until the plants are established. An organic mulch aids in establishment. The plants should be well watered while they are becoming established. They will cover within 1 to 2 years, depending upon the site and the size of the transplants.

After the plants are established, they require annual pruning. The tips can be trimmed at any time to keep the plants within bounds. English Ivy should be heavily pruned in early spring. To maintain dense stands, mow every other spring with a rotary mower raised to its maximum height. Plants can also be rejuvenated by shear ing them close to their bases during the spring.

Fertilize the plants lightly when the leaves begin to lose their healthy dark-green color. Use an acid-type fertilizer in early spring.

Propagation is by layering or by cuttings taken at any time (especially from July through September).

English Ivy is susceptible to leaf spot, stem canker, powdery mildew, root rots, scab, aphids, caterpillars, mealy bugs, scales, and two-spotted mites.

Uses. English Ivy grows well on level ground or on slight slopes. It is especially attractive when planted beneath trees and shrubs. Because this plant is vigorous, it may not be suitable for a small area.

Hedera helix is native to Europe and western Asia, and has become naturalized in parts of the United States. It has long been cultivated.

English Ivy has the ability to produce many sports or mutations, resulting in various leaf shapes, colors, sizes, and degrees of hardiness. Some of these sports also have the ability to revert to their original form, depending upon the stability of the plant. The selections of English Ivy described below can be grown successfully in the Midwest. Selections made by local nurseries may prove equally hardy and well adapted to your area.

'Baltica' has glossy, 1- to 2-inch-long, dark-green leaves with whitish veins. It is originally from Latvia, and was introduced in 1907.

'Bulgaria' reportedly grows well under dry conditions, and has leaves 3 to 4 inches long. It was introduced by the Missouri Botanical Garden in 1953. 'Rumania' is a cultivar similar to 'Bulgaria' except that the leaves are larger.

'Thorndale' has glossy, deep-green leaves with silvery white veins. The leaves are also larger than those of 'Baltica'.

Juniperus chinensis var. *procumbens*

Japgarden Juniper

Zone 4

Cupressaceae (Cypress family)

May be listed as *Juniperus procumbens*

For a color illustration of *Juniperus chinensis* var. *procumbens* 'Nana', see page 59.

J. chinensis var. *procumbens* 'Nana'

Dwarf Japgarden Juniper

Zone 4

Cupressaceae (Cypress family)

May be listed as *Juniperus japonica nana*, *Juniperus procumbens* 'Nana', *Juniperus squamata* var. *prostrata*

stems and leaves (needles)

Japgarden Juniper is a low-growing, uneven, dense, evergreen ground cover that grows 1 to 2 feet high and spreads 10 to 15 feet wide. Growth rate is medium. Texture is fine to medium.

Leaves. The leaves are awl-shaped, ⅓ inch long, and end in a spiny tip. They are borne in groups of 3, and are attached to the stem except at the upper end. The upper leaf surface is concave and bloomy, with a green midrib that runs almost to the tip. The bluish green underside is convex, with two white spots near the base. Two white lines run from the spots down the edge of that part of the leaf attached to the stem. The foliage is bluish to grayish green in all seasons.

Stems. The stiff, ridged branchlets are bloomy and ascend at their tips.

Fruits. The nearly globe-shaped fruits are ⅖ inch wide. They rarely occur on cultivated plants.

Culture. Japgarden Juniper tolerates most well-drained soils, varying from slightly acid to alkaline. It grows best in open areas and full sun. Transplant from containers, and space plants about 2½ feet apart. Japgarden Juniper will tolerate heavy pruning in June and July.

This plant is susceptible to juniper twig blight but shows resistance to cedar apple rust. Two-spotted mites may be troublesome.

Uses. See general discussion of *Juniperus*, page 38.

Juniperus chinensis var. *procumbens* is native to the mountains of Japan. Although introduced in 1843, it was not used widely until after 1903.

Dwarf Japgarden Juniper is an outstanding evergreen ground cover that grows 1 foot high and spreads to 5 feet wide. It is a dwarf, compact, prostrate plant with thick main branches that ascend at their tips. The short, stiff branches grow on top of one another, and vary in length. Growth rate is slow. Texture is fine.

Leaves. The leaves are awl-shaped and shorter and wider than those of the species. They are closely and densely arranged on the stem. The two white spots that appear on the undersides of the leaves of the species are not always visible on the leaves of Dwarf Japgarden Juniper. The new leaves emerge bright green. They become blue-green during the summer, and may assume a slight purplish tinge in the winter.

Culture. Culture is similar to that of *Juniperus chinensis* var. *procumbens* except that the plants should be spaced 1 to 2 feet apart.

Dwarf Japgarden Juniper is moderately susceptible to juniper twig blight.

Uses. See general discussion of *Juniperus*, page 38.

Juniperus chinensis var. *procumbens* 'Nana' was introduced from Japan by D. Hill Nursery, Dundee, Illinois, in 1922.

Juniperus chinensis var. *sargentii*

Sargent's Chinese Juniper

Zone 4

Cupressaceae (Cypress family)

Also known as Sargent's Juniper

May be listed as *Juniperus chinensis* var.
procumbens, Juniperus procumbens

stems and leaves (needles)

Sargent's Chinese Juniper is a prostrate,
matlike, evergreen ground cover that grows from
1 to 2 feet high, and spreads to 10 feet wide.
The long, trailing branches have ascending
branchlets. Growth rate is slow to medium.
Texture is fine to medium.

Leaves. The leaves are scalelike on adult plants,
⅓ inch long, very narrow, and are borne in
whorls of 3. On main branches, the leaves appear
to be separated; on branchlets, they are close
together and loosely pressed to the stem. The
growing tips have a "cordlike" appearance. The
upper leaf surface is concave, with a raised
midrib; the underside is slightly grooved and
bloomy. The foliage is gray-green year-round,
and smells of camphor when crushed. Young
plants have needlelike, grass-green leaves.

Stems. The branches are thick and sturdy;
the branchlets are 4-sided.

Fruits. The slightly bloomy, bluish fruits are
about ¼ inch wide, and are borne in the fall.

Culture. The culture of Sargent's Chinese
Juniper is similar to that of most other junipers.
The plant needs well-drained soil, and will
tolerate salt and poor, dry sites. It should be
grown in full sun. Transplant from containers
and space plants 3 to 6 feet apart.

Sargent's Chinese Juniper is resistant to juniper
twig blight, but is susceptible to cedar apple
rust. Red spider mites may also prove troublesome.

Uses. See general discussion of *Juniperus,*
page 38.

Juniperus chinensis var. *sargentii* was discovered
in 1892 on the coast of the North Island of Japan.
It is also native to other areas of Japan, Korea,
Sakhalin, and the Kuriles.

Juniperus chinensis var. *sargentii* 'Glauca' is a
dwarf cultivar that grows 10 to 18 inches high
and spreads to 10 feet wide. Its thick branches are
covered with bloomy, gray-green foliage.
Growth rate is slow.

Juniperus chinensis var. *sargentii* "Viridis' is
the same size as the variety but lacks its
"bloominess." The foliage remains light green
year-round.

Juniperus chinensis 'San Jose' (San Jose Chinese
Juniper) is a creeping form that grows 1 to 2
feet high and spreads irregularly to 8 feet wide,
lying flat on the ground. Most of the gray-green
leaves are awl-shaped. Plants should be spaced 3
feet apart. San Jose Chinese Juniper was found
in California in 1935. It is somewhat susceptible
to juniper twig blight.

Juniperus communis var. *depressa*

Canadian Juniper

Zone 2

Cupressaceae (Cypress family)

Also known as Oldfield Juniper, Prostrate Juniper

May be listed as *Juniperus canadensis, Juniperus communis* var. *canadensis, Juniperus communis nana canadensis*

Canadian Juniper is a broad, spreading, dense, evergreen ground cover that grows 3 to 5 feet high and spreads 6 to 8 feet wide. The branches grow prostrately, and ascend at the tips. Growth rate is slow to medium. Texture is medium-fine.

Leaves. The awl-shaped leaves are ⅗ inch long and 1/16 inch wide. The tip is long and tapers to a prickly point. The upper surface of the leaf has a broad whitish band down its center; the undersurface is keeled. The leaves at the ends of the strong, growing branches are pressed to the stem, although most leaves remain unpressed.

Culture. Canadian Juniper tolerates dry, rocky, sandy, sterile soil with a wide pH range.

Canadian Juniper grows in full sun to light shade, and tolerates windy sites. If the plant is grown in light shade, the leaves will become less brown in the winter.

Transplant balled-and-burlapped or container-grown plants. Space plants 40 inches apart. Canadian Juniper will tolerate light shearing in June and July.

Uses. See general discussion of *Juniperus,* page 38.

Juniperus communis var. *depressa* is native to eastern North America.

Juniperus conferta

Shore Juniper

Zone 6

Cupressaceae (Cypress family)

For a color illustration of *Juniperus conferta,* see page 59.

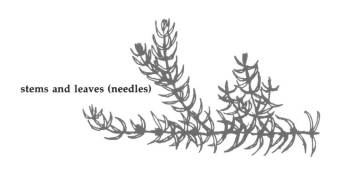

stems and leaves (needles)

Shore Juniper is a dense, procumbent, evergreen ground cover that grows 10 to 18 inches high and spreads to 9 feet wide. This plant will cascade over an embankment or low wall. Growth rate is medium. Texture is fine.

Stems. The thick, trailing branches are gray-brown to reddish brown; the branchlets ascend at their tips.

Fruits. The bloomy, black fruits are almost globe-shaped, ¼ to ½ inch wide, and flat-based. They are abundantly borne in the fall.

Culture. This plant prefers full sun and light, sandy soil. It grows well on slopes and tolerates salt and drouth. Do not plant in heavy or clay soils.

Transplant from container-grown plants. Space plants 2 feet apart. Shore Juniper is subject to winter dieback in cold areas. Prune in June and July.

This plant may suffer from rodent damage in the winter. It is susceptible to juniper twig blight but resistant to cedar apple rust.

Uses. See general discussion of *Juniperus,* page 38.

Juniperus conferta is native to coastal areas of Japan. It was introduced in 1915.

Juniperus horizontalis 'Bar Harbor'

Bar Harbor Creeping Juniper

Zone 3

Cupressaceae (Cypress family)

Juniperus horizontalis 'Douglassii'

Waukegan Creeping Juniper

Zone 3

Cupressaceae (Cypress family)

May be listed as *Juniperus horizontalis glauca major*

stems and leaves (needles)

Bar Harbor Creeping Juniper is a creeping, compact, prostrate, evergreen ground cover that grows 1 foot high and spreads to 10 feet wide. The side branches arise on each side of the stem in a V-shaped pattern. Growth rate is fast. Texture is medium-fine.

Leaves. The leaves are mostly scalelike, small, and loosely pressed to the stems. They are bloomy and gray-green in the summer and turn purplish in the winter, sometimes assuming a brown tinge.

Stems. The young shoots are orange-brown with purple tips, and the main branches are thin and flexible.

Fruits. Fruits are rarely borne in cultivation.

Culture. This plant tolerates hard pruning, and is susceptible to juniper twig blight.

Uses. See general discussion of *Juniperus*, page 38.

Juniperus horizontalis 'Bar Harbor' is native to Mount Desert Island, Maine.

Waukegan Creeping Juniper is a dense, low-growing, trailing, evergreen ground cover that grows ½ to 1½ feet high and spreads to 10 feet wide. The main branches hug the ground, and the sprays of needles grow upright from either side of the stem in a U-shaped pattern. Growth rate is medium to fast. Texture is fine.

Leaves. The leaves are both awl-shaped and scalelike. The juvenile awl-shaped leaves are densely overlapping, giving the branchlets a tufted appearance. The leaves are bloomy and a bright gray-green in the summer, becoming purplish in the winter.

Culture. Waukegan Creeping Juniper will tolerate light shade. Space plants about 5 feet apart.

This plant is susceptible to both juniper twig blight and cedar apple rust.

Uses. See general discussion of *Juniperus*, page 38.

Juniperus horizontalis 'Douglasii' was found near the old Douglas Nursery in Waukegan, Illinois, before 1855.

Juniperus horizontalis 'Plumosa'

Andorra Creeping Juniper

Zone 4

Cupressaceae (Cypress family)

May be listed as *Juniperus horizontalis* var. *depressa plumosa*

For a color illustration of *Juniperus horizontalis* 'Plumosa', see page 59.

stems and leaves (needles)

Andorra Creeping Juniper is a flat-topped, spreading, evergreen ground cover that grows to 1½ feet high and spreads to 8 feet wide. The branches have a plumelike appearance. They grow in all directions from the center of the plant, with the branchlets arising at a 45-degree angle. Growth rate is medium to fast. Texture is fine.

Leaves. The leaves are mostly awl-shaped, ⅙ inch long, and loosely pressed to the stem. They are gray-green during the growing season, becoming purplish in the winter.

Culture. Winter tip burn may occur in cold areas, and the plant may not cover densely. In warmer areas, Andorra Creeping Juniper is usually dense growing.

This plant is susceptible to juniper twig blight and cedar apple rust.

Uses. See general discussion of *Juniperus,* page 38.

Juniperus horizontalis 'Plumosa' was introduced in 1919 by the Andorra Nurseries of Philadelphia.

Several selections of *Juniperus horizontalis* 'Plumosa' are available, including *Juniperus horizontalis* 'Plumosa Compacta' (Compact Andorra Creeping Juniper) and *Juniperus horizontalis* 'Plumosa Compacta Youngstownii' (Youngstown Compact Creeping Juniper). Compact Andorra Creeping Juniper grows to about 1 foot high and spreads to 8 feet wide. Although this plant is slower growing and more compact than Andorra Creeping Juniper, it also has rising branchlets and is gray-green during the summer and purplish in the winter. Youngstown Compact Creeping Juniper is similar to Compact Andorra Creeping Juniper, but usually remains green during the winter.

Juniperus horizontalis 'Wiltonii'

Blue Rug Creeping Juniper

Zone 4

Cupressaceae (Cypress family)

Also known as Blue Wilton Creeping Juniper, Wilton Carpet Creeping Juniper, Wilton's Creeping Juniper

May be listed as *Juniperus horizontalis* 'Blue Rug', *Juniperus horizontalis* 'Blue Wilton', *Juniperus horizontalis* 'Glauca', *Juniperus horizontalis* 'Glauca Nana', *Juniperus horizontalis* 'Wilton Carpet'

For a color illustration of *Juniperus horizontalis* 'Wiltonii', see page 59.

stems, leaves (needles), and fruits

Blue Rug Creeping Juniper is a prostrate, dense, flat, evergreen ground cover that grows 6 to 8 inches high and spreads 6 to 8 feet wide. This plant is the lowest growing of the junipers. The branchlets are long and slender, and may occasionally take root. Growth rate is slow. Texture is fine.

Leaves. The leaves are small and closely pressed to the stem. They are silvery blue in the summer, and may assume a gray-blue to slightly purplish tinge in the winter.

Fruits. The fairly abundant blue fruits are ⅓ inch in diameter, and are borne on recurved stalks.

Culture. Space plants 3 to 5 feet apart. Because of its extremely low height, Blue Rug Creeping Juniper may have trouble competing with weeds and other plants. It should be planted in areas where weeds can be controlled. Mulch is helpful in keeping weed growth to a minimum.

This plant is susceptible to juniper twig blight but resistant to cedar apple rust.

Uses. See general discussion of *Juniperus*, page 38.

Juniperus horizontalis 'Wiltonii' was discovered in 1914 on Vinalhaven Island, Maine.

Juniperus sabina selections

Zone 3

Cupressaceae (Cypress family)

stems and leaves (needles)

The species *Juniperus sabina* (Savin Juniper) is not suitable for a ground cover, but the selections of the species described below can be used as ground covers in the Midwest. For the culture of these selections, see the general discussion of *Juniperus,* page 38.

Juniperus sabina 'Tamariscifolia' (Tamarisk Juniper) is a spreading, flat-topped, mounded, evergreen ground cover that grows less than 4 feet high and spreads widely. The branches grow horizontally, and may eventually arch slightly. The branchlets are densely produced, and arise from the branches in V-shaped sprays. Growth rate is slow. Texture is fine.

The bright, bluish green leaves are awl-shaped, short, and sharp-pointed. They are usually arranged oppositely on the stem, but may be whorled in groups of 3. The leaves are densely produced, and are crowded on the stem. They are slightly pressed to the stem, being free near the apex; the apex may be incurved. The upper leaf surface is banded in white, and the lower surface usually has a gland.

This plant may be susceptible to juniper twig blight.

Juniperus sabina 'Tamariscifolia' is native to the mountains of southern Europe. It has long been cultivated.

Juniperus sabina 'Arcadia' (Arcadia Savin Juniper) is a dense, dwarf evergreen ground cover that grows 20 inches high and spreads to 7 feet wide. The branches spread horizontally, and may arch, causing the plant to resemble the Tamarisk

Juniper. The leaves are mostly scalelike and grass green in color. They may yellow somewhat in the winter. Growth rate is fairly fast.

Juniperus sabina 'Broadmoor' (Broadmoor Savin Juniper) is a spreading, evergreen ground cover that grows 1 to 2 feet high and can spread to more than 9 feet wide. The horizontal branches have short, upturned branchlets. As the plant grows, it may build up in its center. The grayish green leaves are ⅟₁₆ inch long. Broadmoor Savin Juniper is a male selection, and does not produce fruits. Growth rate is fairly fast.

Juniperus sabina 'Skandia' (Skandia Savin Juniper) is a low, prostrate, flat-topped, dense, evergreen ground cover that grows 1 foot high and spreads to 9 feet wide. The needle-shaped leaves are grayish to medium green, and may yellow slightly in winter.

Juniperus sabina 'Arcadia', 'Broadmoor', and 'Skandia' originated as seedlings raised by the D. Hill Nursery, Dundee, Illinois. They were selected in 1933, and the seed was imported from near the Ural Mountains in Russia. All three of these selections are very hardy and resistant to juniper twig blight.

Juniperus squamata 'Prostrata'

Prostrate Singleseed Juniper

Zone 4

Cupressaceae (Cypress family)

May be listed as *Juniperus procumbens prostrata*

stems and leaves (needles)

Prostrate Singleseed Juniper is a low-growing, prostrate, evergreen ground cover. The branchlets can be horizontally spreading or very short and erect. They grow in wide fans, and the tips turn downwards. Growth rate is slow.

Leaves. The narrow, awl-shaped leaves are ⅙ to ¼ inch long. They can be straight or curved, with finely pointed tips. The upper leaf surface is green, with broad margins and two grayish or bluish white bands; the convex lower surface is also green, and can be grooved from the base to near the tip. The leaves are loosely pressed to the branchlet, and persist as dry, brown scales.

Stems. The stems are green, thick, and grooved.

Culture. See general discussion of *Juniperus,* page 38.

Uses. See general discussion of *Juniperus,* page 38.

Juniperus squamata 'Prostrata' was introduced in 1909.

General Discussion of *Juniperus* (Junipers)

The junipers are a variable group of plants ranging from spreading ground covers 6 inches high to upright trees over 50 feet high.

Junipers can have both needlelike (awl-shaped) leaves and scalelike leaves. Juvenile plants have needlelike leaves; more mature plants may have both needlelike and scalelike leaves. Foliage color ranges from yellow-green to bright green to gray- or blue-green.

Junipers adapt well to almost any well-drained soil. Some of these plants can tolerate sandy sites, and several are salt-tolerant. Most junipers will tolerate drouth.

The preferred exposure is full sun in open locations. Some junipers tolerate light shade, but they may become quite woody and open, with reduced foliage color. Many of these plants tolerate city conditions and air pollution.

Balled-and-burlapped or container-grown plants can be transplanted. Most of the low, spreading junipers are available as container-grown plants, and these are usually the easiest to transplant. Junipers should not be planted too close together; most of the selections described in this book should be planted 2½ to 5 feet apart. An organic mulch applied at planting will aid in establishment.

After junipers are established, they usually require little fertilization. If foliage color fades or yellows, a light application of an organic fertilizer (cottonseed meal or soybean meal) is recommended. Mix the fertilizer lightly into the mulch in the spring.

Most junipers can withstand pruning. Prune lightly in June and July. The plants can be shaped at this time, and long, trailing branches can be cut back to vigorous side branches.

Never leave stubs when pruning. Remove large branches in mid-April. Prune back to a lateral branch or crotch. Some of the ground cover junipers may develop dead areas in their centers. Do not expose these areas when pruning unless green leaves are present. If there are no green leaves, the branches may not produce shoots, and a dead brown area may be permanently exposed.

Most of the junipers described in this book are dense enough to discourage weed growth. Mulch not only keeps weeds to a minimum but enhances the appearance of the bed. Weeds can also be removed by hand or through the use of herbicides.

Junipers are susceptible to many diseases and insect pests, including twig blight, cedar apple rust, wilt, Rocky Mountain juniper aphids, bagworms, juniper midges, juniper scale, juniper webworm-redcedar bark beetles, and two-spotted mites. Juniper twig blight, bagworms, and two-spotted mites have been serious problems in the Midwest. For those plants that are not resistant, chemical controls are available. Ask your county Extension adviser for pesticide (herbicide, insecticide, and fungicide) recommendations.

Propagation is by seeds, grafting, and cuttings taken from November through February.

Junipers can be used in both large and small areas if they are pruned to keep them within bounds. Because these plants grow well on slopes, they have long been recommended as erosion controls. They rarely form large root masses, however, and do not bind the soil adequately. If junipers are planted close enough together to control erosion on slopes, the natural appearance of the plant is destroyed.

Lonicera japonica 'Halliana'

Hall's Honeysuckle

Zone 4

Caprifoliaceae (Honeysuckle family)

May be listed as *Lonicera flexuosa* 'Halliana', *Lonicera halliana*

For color illustrations of *Lonicerea alpigena* 'Nana', *Lonicera japonica* 'Aureo-reticulata', and *Lonicera sempervirens*, see page 60.

leaves and flowers

Hall's Honeysuckle is an extremely vigorous, climbing, twining, semievergreen vine ground cover that grows 2 feet high and has an almost unlimited spread. If unchecked, this plant can mound on itself to a height of 6 feet. If shrubs, trees, or other objects are in its path, it can climb from 15 to 30 feet high. The creeping branches root wherever they touch moist soil, and a branch can grow up to 15 feet in length during a single growing season. Growth rate is fast. Texture is medium-coarse.

Leaves. The leaves are opposite, simple, and 1½ to 3½ inches long, with a ⅕-inch-long leafstalk. The leaf varies from egg-shaped to linear with nearly parallel sides. The apex is commonly pointed, and the base can be rounded to almost heart-shaped. The margins are entire (rarely lobed), and occasionally fringed with hair. Both upper and lower leaf surfaces are usually hairy. The foliage is a dark green during the growing season, turning bronze in cool weather.

Stems. The twining, light brown to reddish brown stems are usually hairy, wiry, and hollow.

Flowers. The trumpet-shaped, fragrant, pure white flowers turn yellow with age, and are borne in pairs in the leaf axils from May through September. The flowers are perfect, about 1 to 1½ inches long, and irregularly divided or 2-lipped. The upper lip is divided nearly to its midpoint. Leafy bracts grow beneath the flowers. The floral stalks are usually longer than the leafstalks.

Fruits. The fruits are nearly globose black berries that are ⅕ inch wide. They are borne from September through October, and are not ornamental.

Culture. Hall's Honeysuckle grows best in a rich, well-drained, loamy, cool soil. It will, however, grow in almost any soil with a pH range from 4 to 8, and will tolerate drouth.

This plant grows well in full sun to partial shade, and tolerates windy conditions.

Hall's Honeysuckle can quickly grow out of bounds, and has become a nuisance where it has escaped cultivation in parts of southern Pennsylvania, Maryland, and Virginia. The plant climbs by twining, and can kill shrubs and small trees. It can be especially dangerous around new plantings.

Hall's Honeysuckle is easy to transplant in either the fall or spring. Spacing depends upon the area in which it is used. On level ground, the plants should be spaced from 1 to 6 feet apart; on slopes, they can be spaced from 1 to 3 feet apart. After the plants are established, prune annually in early spring. Apply a complete fertilizer in the spring if the plants are growing on extremely poor sites; otherwise, no fertilization is necessary.

Propagation is by division, layering, or stem cuttings.

Hall's Honeysuckle is susceptible to several diseases and insect pests, including aphids.

Uses. Hall's Honeysuckle should be planted only in large areas where it cannot invade or take over. It can be used effectively on steep slopes, banks, and in other areas in which it is difficult to grow other plants.

Lonicera japonica 'Halliana' is native to eastern Asia. It has escaped cultivation and become naturalized in the United States south of a line from Massachusetts to Kansas. This plant was introduced before 1860.

In addition to *Lonicera japonica* 'Halliana', the honeysuckles described below are suitable for use as ground covers in the Midwest.

Lonicera alpigena 'Nana' (Dwarf Alps Honeysuckle) is a small, upright, rounded, shrubby plant that grows up to 3 feet high. The large leaves are lustrous above and pubescent beneath. The dark reddish flowers are borne in pairs on upright, hairy stalks in mid-May, and are not showy. The ornamental red fruits are about ½ inch long, and are borne in late summer. For best flowering and fruiting, Dwarf Alps Honeysuckle should be grown in full sun.

Lonicera japonica 'Aureo-reticulata' (Yellownet Honeysuckle) is similar to Hall's Honeysuckle except that the leaves are smaller (usually no longer than 2 inches), and are bright green with conspicuous yellow or gold netting throughout. The plant also produces fewer flowers and is less vigorous and cold hardy than Hall's Honeysuckle. It grows best in full sun.

Lonicera henryi (Henry Honeysuckle) is a hardy, twining or prostrate, semievergreen vine that does not grow as rampantly as Hall's Honeysuckle. The dark-green leaves are opposite, oval, 2 to 3 inches long, and have hairy margins. The trumpet-shaped flowers are yellowish to reddish purple, ½ to ¾ inch long, and short stalked. They are borne in pairs from June through August, and are often bunched toward the stem tips. The berrylike black fruits often persist into early winter. *Lonicera henryi* is native to China.

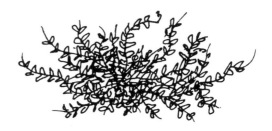

Lonicera sempervirens (Trumpet Honeysuckle) is a climbing, twining, semievergreen to evergreen vine that can climb higher than 20 feet. The leaves are opposite, oval, and 1 to 3¼ inches long. They are red or purple when they emerge, later turning bluish green. The last 1 or 2 pairs of leaves on the vine are joined at the base; the leaf completely encircles the stem. The trumpet-shaped flowers are 2 inches long, and are borne in terminal clusters from June through August. The flowers are usually orange to scarlet on the outside and yellow or orange inside, and are not fragrant. Selections have been made for scarlet or yellow flowering forms. The bright red, ¼-inch-wide fruits ripen in September.

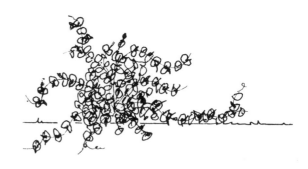

Mahonia repens

Creeping Mahonia

Zone 5

Berberidaceae (Barberry family)

Also known as Ash Barberry, Creeping Hollygrape, Dwarf Hollygrape

May be listed as *Berberis aquifolium, Berberis nana, Berberis repens, Odostemon aquifolium*

For a color illustration of *Mahonia repens,* see page 60.

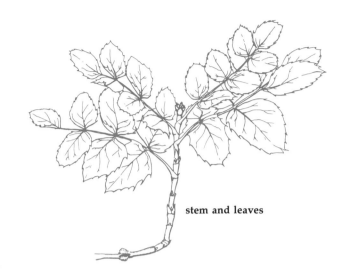

stem and leaves

Creeping Mahonia is a stiff, colonizing, evergreen to semievergreen ground cover that grows to 1 foot high and spreads by underground stems. Growth rate is medium. Texture is medium-coarse.

Leaves. The leaves are alternate and odd-pinnate (3, 5, or 7 leaflets), with a leafstalk up to 3 inches long. The oval, leathery leaflets are 1 to 3 inches long. The margins have from 6 to 14 fine, bristly tipped teeth per side, and appear hollylike. The lateral leaflets do not have stalks. The upper surfaces of the leaves are dull blue-green, and the undersides are gray-green with tiny, nipplelike projections.

Flowers. The small, fragrant, deep yellow flowers are perfect and have 6 petals. They are borne in dense, erect, 1- to 3-inch clusters from April through June.

Fruits. The fruits are black berries about ¼ inch in diameter that are covered with a blue bloom. They are borne in grapelike clusters from June through September.

Culture. Creeping Mahonia prefers a moist, well-drained, slightly acid soil. It will, however, grow in a wide variety of good soils that have been supplemented with organic matter.

Proper siting is important. Creeping Mahonia can tolerate full sun in all but very hot and dry areas, but it must be protected from winter wind and sun that can damage the foliage. Partial shade is desirable to minimize the effects of winter sun and wind.

Creeping Mahonia can be difficult to transplant. Creeping shoots, balled-and-burlapped plants, or container-grown plants can be transplanted. Plant in the spring or early fall. Space plants 10 to 24 inches apart. Mulching and thorough watering will help in establishment. Prune in the spring. If fertilizer is needed, add an acid-balanced fertilizer at the same time.

Propagation is by seeds, division, root cuttings, and stem cuttings of half-ripe wood. This plant is not seriously affected by insect pests or diseases.

Uses. Creeping Mahonia can be used effectively in rock gardens and in small and naturalized areas. The flowers, fruits, and foliage are attractive, and the plant should be placed where it can easily be seen. Because Creeping Mahonia may open in the center, it should not be planted in large areas.

Mahonia repens is native to British Columbia south to California and northern Mexico. It was introduced in 1822.

Mahonia nervosa (Cascade Mahonia) is a related species of Creeping Mahonia, and some nurseries sell these two plants interchangeably. Cascade Mahonia grows up to 2 feet high, and is evergreen. The culture is similar to that of *Mahonia repens* except that Cascade Mahonia requires an acid soil and more winter protection because it is more prone to burn. Plants should be spaced 2 feet apart.

41

Mitchella repens

Partridgeberry

Zone 3

Rubiaceae (Madder family)

Also known as Running Box, Squawberry, Squawvine, Twinberry, Two-Eyed Berry

For a color illustration of *Mitchella repens*, see page 60.

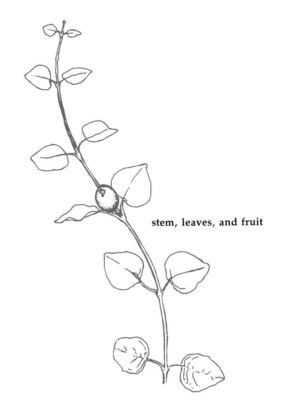

stem, leaves, and fruit

Partridgeberry is a creeping, prostrate, mat-forming, evergreen ground cover that grows 1 to 6 inches high and spreads 1 to 2 feet wide. The branchlets root as they spread, and are barely woody. Growth rate is slow. Texture is fine.

Leaves. The leaves are opposite, simple, and ¼ to 1 inch long, with a short leafstalk. The leaf is circular to egg-shaped (wider toward the base), with a rounded to blunt apex and a curved or heart-shaped base. The margins are entire. The leaves are a lustrous dark green, with white veins or lines.

Stems. The stems are slender, glabrous (without hairs) or slightly hairy, and up to 1 foot in length.

Flowers. The funnel-shaped, fragrant, white or white-tinged pink or purple flowers occur in terminal pairs from May through July. The flowers are perfect, about ⅖ to ½ inch long, and have 4 recurved lobes and a short flower stalk. The lobes are hairy inside. Flowers and fruit can occur on the plant at the same time.

Fruits. The fruits are scarlet berries that appear from summer into winter, and are eaten by wildlife. They are globose, about ¼ inch in diameter, and have 8 roundish nutlets.

Culture. Partridgeberry grows best in a cool, moist, well-drained, acid soil. Organic matter should be added to heavy soils.

This plant is native to woodlands, and does not grow well in full sun. Cool summer temperatures are required for it to maintain good health.

Partridgeberry is not a rugged plant, and unless it is planted in a shady site with the proper soil, it is difficult to establish. Transplant in sods, leaving as much soil as possible. Rooted runners may also be transplanted. Plant in the spring, and make sure that the soil does not dry out while the plants are becoming established. An organic mulch is helpful. Partridgeberry is commonly seen in terrariums.

Propagation is by seeds, division, and cuttings.

This plant is not seriously affected by insect pests or diseases.

Uses. Partridgeberry is attractive thoughout the year, and should be planted where it can be seen. It is especially effective in naturalized areas beneath trees and shrubs. This plant is well worth the effort necessary to grow it successfully.

Mitchella repens is native to eastern North America, from Nova Scotia to Minnesota and south to Florida and Texas. It was introduced in 1761.

Pachysandra terminalis

Japanese Spurge

Zone 4

Buxaceae (Boxwood family)

Also known as Japanese Pachysandra

For a color illustration of *Pachysandra terminalis* 'Green Carpet', see page 61.

stems, leaves, and flowers

Japanese Spurge is a neat, uniform, evergreen ground cover that grows ½ to 1 foot high. It spreads by underground stems, and forms a dense mat. Growth rate is medium. Texture is medium.

Leaves. The leaves are alternate (although they tend to cluster toward the apex of the stem and appear whorled), simple, and 1½ to 4 inches long, with a leafstalk ⅖ to 1⅕ inches long. The leaf blade is usually wider beyond its center, with a somewhat blunt to pointed apex and a wedge-shaped base. The margin on the upper ½ of the leaf is coarsely toothed; the lower margin is usually entire. The leaves are hairless and thick in texture. The new leaves emerge a light green, becoming a dark, lustrous green at maturity.

Stems. The greenish to tannish stems are upright.

Flowers. The small, fragrant flowers are borne above the leaves in erect, 1- to 2-inch spikes in late March through early May. They are not showy, and are sparsely produced.

Fruits. The inconspicuous, ovoid, white, berry-like fruits are about ⅓ inch in diameter, and appear after the flowers.

Culture. Japanese Spurge grows well in organic, moist, acidic to neutral, well-drained soil with a pH of 5 to 7.

This plant is one of the best ground covers for shady sites; full sun causes the leaves to yellow. It requires protection from winter sun and wind, and will not tolerate foot traffic.

Transplant container-grown plants. Space plants ½ to 1 foot apart. (With the 1-foot spacing, Japanese Spurge will not cover fully for 2 to 3 years.) After the plants are established, pinch annually in the spring to encourage branching and a denser bed. Do not shear the plants to the ground.

Japanese Spurge will not tolerate drouth, and mulching will help maintain an adequate moisture level throughout the growing season. This plant grows well in fertile soils. Add a complete fertilizer to the soil in the spring.

Propagation is by division in the spring, rooted stolons, or cuttings taken in early summer.

Japanese Spurge is susceptible to several insect pests and diseases, including scales, mites, leaf tier, stem canker, and leaf blight. A vigorous stand of plants will help combat these problems.

Uses. Japanese Spurge can be used on slopes or on level ground in protected locations. It is especially attractive beneath trees or shrubs.

Pachysandra terminalis is native to Japan, and was introduced in 1882.

Two cultivars of *Pachysandra terminalis* are worth considering — *Pachysandra terminalis* 'Variegata' and *Pachysandra terminalis* 'Green Carpet'. 'Variegata' ('Silveredge') has white, variegated leaves. It is less hardy and vigorous than the species, and should be grown in deep shade. 'Green Carpet' is an extremely uniform, dark-green ground cover. It has slightly shorter leaves and is somewhat lower than the species.

Paxistima canbyi

Canby Paxistima

Zone 5

Celastraceae (Staff-tree family)

Also known as Canby Pachistima, Canby's Pachistima, Canby's Paxistima, Cliff-Green, Mountain-Lover, Pachistima, Paxistima, Rat-Stripper

May be listed as *Pachistima canbyi, Pachystima canbyi*

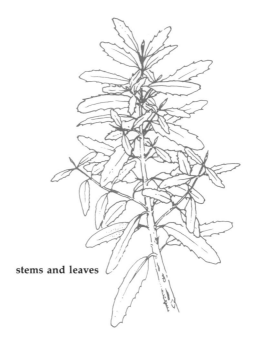

stems and leaves

Canby Paxistima is a dense, creeping, clump-forming, evergreen ground cover that grows 1 to 1½ feet high and spreads 2 to 4 feet wide. The branchlets root as they spread, and turn up at their ends. Growth rate is slow to medium. Texture is fine.

Leaves. The leaves are opposite, simple, and ¼ to 1 inch long, with a short leafstalk. The leaf is linear, with nearly parallel sides that are commonly less than ¼ inch apart and a squared apex. The margins roll downward, and small serrations usually occur beyond the middle of the leaf (the margins are rarely entire). The hairless leaves are lustrous dark green, turning bronze as the weather cools.

Stems. The slender stems are 4-sided and warty, with a spongy pith. As the bark ages, it becomes thicker and corky, with transverse checks.

Flowers. The inconspicuous reddish flowers are perfect, 4-petaled, and about ⅕ inch wide and ⅓ inch long, with a flower stalk ⅛ to ¼ inch long. They are borne in axillary clusters from late April through early May.

Fruits. The fruits are small, leathery, white capsules about ⅙ inch long and ³⁄₁₆ inch wide. They have 1 or 2 seeds, and are of no ornamental value.

Culture. Canby Paxistima occurs naturally on rocky slopes, but grows well in any moist, acid, well-drained soil with a pH from 4.5 to 6. A higher soil pH can cause foliar discoloration and slow growth. Although the branches root as they spread, Canby Paxistima is not considered a suitable plant for controlling soil erosion. If grown in a poorly drained soil, the plant may die. It should not be used in beds that are frequently irrigated.

Canby Paxistima grows well in full sun to partial shade, although winter sun can damage the foliage. It can be grown north of Zone 5 if there is adequate snow cover for insulation.

Canby Paxistima is easy to transplant from container-grown plants. Space plants 12 to 14 inches apart. Two-year-old transplants usually require 2 years to cover. Transplant in the spring, and keep the plants moist until they are established. Mulching aids in establishment. Once established, Canby Paxistima requires little maintenance, and rarely needs pruning or fertilizing.

Propagation is by seeds, division in the spring, layering, and cuttings. Cuttings can be taken from half-hardened wood in midsummer or from hardwood in the fall.

This plant is not seriously affected by insect pests and diseases, although scale and leaf spot have been reported.

Uses. Canby Paxistima can be used effectively beneath trees and shrubs and as a low hedge or border for a walkway.

Paxistima canbyi is native to the mountains of Virginia and West Virginia, and has been in cultivation since 1880.

Rhus aromatica 'Gro-Low'

Gro-Low Fragrant Sumac

Zone 3

Anacardiaceae (Cashew family)

For a color illustration of *Rhus aromatica* 'Gro-Low', see page 61.

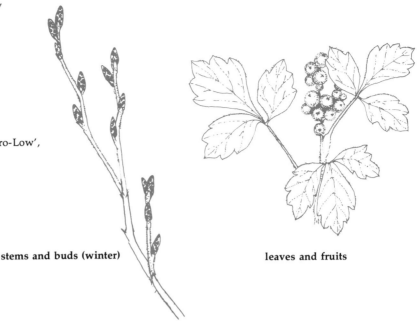

stems and buds (winter)   leaves and fruits

Gro-Low Fragrant Sumac is a low-growing, spreading, deciduous ground cover that grows 2 to 4 feet high and spreads to 12 feet wide in cool areas. The plant may spread by both underground stems and aboveground rooting branches. The branches can become dense and tangled. Growth rate is medium. Texture is medium in leaf, becoming coarse after the leaves drop.

Leaves. The leaves are alternate, trifoliolate (3 leaflets), and 2 to 5 inches long, with a ½- to ¼-inch leafstalk. The leaflets are 1 to 3 inches long, coarsely toothed, oval, and pointed at the apex. The terminal leaflet has a rounded or wedge-shaped base; it may also have a leaf stalklet, and is commonly the largest of the 3 leaflets. The 2 lateral leaflets usually have a rounded base and are unstalked. The leaves are hairy, especially when young. They are a glossy medium-blue green, and may turn yellow to scarlet in the fall. Autumn coloration is best on light, well-drained soils or in full sun. When bruised, the leaves are aromatic.

Stems. The stems are slender, hairy, and fragrant when crushed.

Flowers. *Rhus aromatica* may bear only staminate (male) flowers, only pistillate (female) flowers, both perfect and male flowers, and both perfect and female flowers. The male flowers are borne in late summer; they persist as catkins until they open in March or April. The female flowers are clustered at the branch ends, and open at the same time as the male flowers. The flowers are yellowish

Fruits. The hairy, globe-shaped, red fruits are about ¼ inch in diameter. They are borne in small, upright clusters from August through September, and may be eaten by wildlife.

Culture. Gro-Low Fragrant Sumac will grow in both sun and shade in almost any soil, although it grows best in poor, dry, well-drained soils. This plant is salt-tolerant.

Transplant at any time with container-grown plants. Space plants 2 to 3 feet apart. After the plants have become established, they can be pruned in early spring. Shearing to 6 inches results in a denser cover. One to 2 years are required for the plant to regrow. The branches are weak and brittle, and it may be necessary to prune dead wood.

Propagation is by root division in the fall or spring, layering, and softwood cuttings taken in July.

This plant is not seriously affected by insect pests or diseases.

Uses. Gro-Low Fragrant Sumac is more attractive in large areas than in small ones, and less pruning is required to keep it within bounds. It can also be used as an erosion control on slopes and banks.

Rhus aromatica 'Gro-Low' was introduced by the Burr Oak Nursery (Ralph Synnestvedt and Associates, Inc., Glenview, Illinois). This plant is patented.

45

Salix purpurea 'Nana'

Dwarf Arctic Willow

Zone 4

Salicaceae (Willow family)

Also known as Dwarf Blue-leaved Arctic Willow, Dwarf Purple Osier Willow

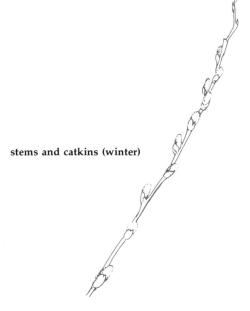

stems and catkins (winter)

Dwarf Arctic Willow is a compact, dense, bushy, deciduous ground cover that grows 3 to 4 feet high. Growth rate is fast. Texture is medium-fine in leaf, becoming coarser after the leaves have dropped.

Leaves. The blue-green leaves are densely borne, narrow, and 1 to 1½ inches long.

Stems. The stems are slender and erect, and may vary in color from purplish to light grayish brown.

Flowers. The flowers are small, gray catkins that appear in March. The male catkins have yellow anthers.

Culture. Dwarf Arctic Willow is a hardy, easy-to-grow plant for low, moist areas. It grows best in full sun. Space plants 1½ to 2 feet apart. This plant withstands heavy shearing, and is often used as a low-sheared hedge. Prune in the spring after the flowers have bloomed. To promote denser growth, prune the entire plant to 4 to 6 inches high every two years.

Dwarf Arctic Willow is susceptible to the insect pests and diseases that attack willows (see *Salix tristis,* page 48). Powdery mildew can be especially troublesome.

Uses. See *Salix tristis,* page 48.

The species *Salix purpurea* is native to Europe, north Africa, central Asia, and Japan, and has become naturalized in the United States. In certain areas, *Salix purpurea* 'Gracilis' may be sold as a cultivar identical with *Salix purpurea* 'Nana'.

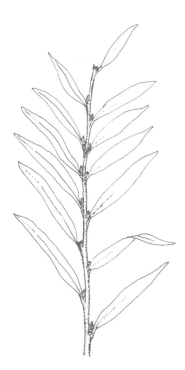

leaves and buds

Salix repens

Creeping Willow

Zone 4

Salicaceae (Willow family)

For a color illustration of *Salix repens* 'Nitida', see page 61.

stems and buds (winter)

Creeping Willow is a prostrate, deciduous ground cover that grows 3 feet high and spreads widely by underground stems, forming large, dense clumps. These stems arise erectly at their tips.

Leaves. The leaves are alternate, simple, and ¾ to 2 inches long, with a short leafstalk. The leaf is narrowly oval, with a recurved, pointed or rounded apex. The margin is entire or very slightly toothed, and rolls downward. The leaves emerge hairy; the upper surfaces may lose their hair as the leaves mature. The under surfaces are a grayish green-white.

Stems. The stems are hairy when young, later becoming hairless and brown with reddish or purplish highlights.

Flowers. The short-stalked flowers are borne before or with the leaves in the spring. The male flowers are ⅖ to ⅗ inch long; the female flowers are about 1⅖ inches long. The male flowers have showy, yellow anthers.

Culture. Creeping Willow grows best in poor, moist-to-wet soils. If grown in rich soils, it becomes leggy and overgrown. This plant should be grown in full sun to light shade.

Creeping Willow is susceptible to the insect pests and diseases that attack willows (see *Salix tristis*, page 48).

Uses. See *Salix tristis*, page 48.

Salix repens is native to Europe and west to northeastern Asia.

Salix repens var. *argentea* (*Salix repens* 'Nitida') is a selection of *Salix repens*. The broadly oval leaves are silvery green above and a lighter green beneath. Both surfaces are pubescent. This plant is quite handsome in leaf.

stem and leaves

Salix tristis

Dwarf Gray Willow

Zone 2

Salicaceae (Willow family)

Also known as Dwarf Prairie Willow, Dwarf Pussy Willow, Prairie Willow, Sage Willow

May be listed as *Salix humilis* var. *microphylla*

stems and leaves

Dwarf Gray Willow is a low, shrubby, deciduous ground cover that grows 1½ to 4 feet high. Growth rate is slow. Texture is medium to medium-fine.

Leaves. The leaves are alternate (or may be clustered at the ends of the twigs), simple, and ½ to 2 inches long, with a short leafstalk. The leaf is narrowly oval, with a pointed or slightly blunted apex and a wedge-shaped base. The margins are entire or slightly toothed, and roll downwards. The leaves are gray-green above and gray and densely hairy beneath. Mature leaves have a thick texture.

Stems. The young stems are gray and hairy; mature stems lose their hair. The twigs and buds serve as food for wildlife.

Flowers. The flowers are short, oval or rounded catkins that appear briefly from April through May before or with the leaves.

Fruits. The fruits are tiny capsules ¼ to ⅓ inch long that appear from May through June. They are not showy.

Culture. The Dwarf Gray Willow grows best in full sun in dry, sandy soil. It tolerates light shade and windy areas.

Dwarf Gray Willow should be transplanted in the spring. Space plants 2 to 3 feet apart. Prune in the spring following flowering.

Propagation is by layering, division, and softwood, semihardwood, or hardwood cuttings.

Many diseases attack willows, including bacterial twig blight, crown gall, leaf blight, black canker, gray scab, leaf spot, powdery mildew, rust, and tar spot. Insect pests include aphids, pine cone gall, basket willow gall, willow lace bug, willow flea weevil, mottled willow borer, poplar borer, willow shoot saw fly, and willow scurfy scale.

Uses. Willows should not be used in small, formal areas because they are too coarse and not dense enough. They are most effective in large or naturalized areas. Willows grow well on slopes, and can be used to control erosion.

Salix tristis is native from Maine west to Minnesota and Montana, and south to northern Florida and northern Oklahoma. It was introduced in 1765.

Salix apoda is another willow that is suitable for use in dry areas. This deciduous, prostrate shrub has glossy green leaves that are paler green beneath. The stems hug the ground as the plant creeps. Before the leaves appear, the silvery, furry male catkins expand and become showy. These catkins are 1 to 1¼ inches long, and are borne upright along the stems. The anthers are bright yellow. This plant is effective in rock gardens or rocky sites at the base of a slope. Leaf diseases can be especially troublesome in humid areas, and may cause defoliation. *Salix apoda* is native to the Caucasus, a mountain range in southern Europe. It was introduced in 1939, but is not yet well-known in cultivation.

Stephanandra incisa 'Crispa'

Dwarf Cutleaf Stephanandra

Zone 5

Rosaceae (Rose family)

Also known as Crisped Stephanandra

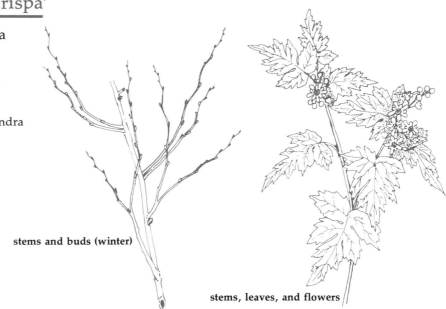

stems and buds (winter)

stems, leaves, and flowers

Dwarf Cutleaf Stephanandra is a mounded, dense, deciduous ground cover that grows 1½ to 3 feet high and spreads to 4 feet wide. The graceful, arching branches root wherever they touch soil. Growth rate is fast. Texture is fine in leaf, becoming somewhat coarser after the leaves have dropped.

Leaves. The leaves are alternate, simple, stipulate, and ⅘ to 1⅘ inches long, with ⅛- to ⅖-inch leafstalks. They are borne on short shoots up to 3 inches long, and usually occur in two rows along the stems. The leaf is a triangular oval shape, with a long, pointed apex and a heart-shaped or squared-off base. The margin is both toothed and deeply lobed. The veins on the underside of the leaf may be hairy. The leaves emerge tinged red, becoming bright green during the summer and red-orange to red-purple in the fall.

Stems. The slender, cinnamon-brown stems are zigzag and somewhat 3- or 5-sided in cross-section.

Flowers. The greenish white flowers are ⅙ to ⅕ inch wide, and are borne in loose, terminal clusters in early June. The clusters are 1 to 2½ inches long, and are not showy.

Fruits. The fruits are small, dry, lopsided follicles that are not ornamental.

Culture. Dwarf Cutleaf Stephanandra grows best in organic, moist, acid, well-drained soils. If the soil becomes too dry, the plant may die. Chlorosis may be a problem in soils that are too alkaline.

Although full sun is preferable, Dwarf Cutleaf Stephanandra will grow in light shade. This plant should be protected from winter winds that can kill young branches.

Dwarf Cutleaf Stephanandra can be transplanted at any time provided that adequate moisture is available during hot, dry periods. Use container-grown plants. Space plants 1 to 2 feet apart. An organic mulch aids in establishment. Prune in early spring before new growth starts. Young branches are susceptible to damage from winter winds and severe cold, and should also be pruned in early spring. Removing several of the largest branches helps to keep the plant dense and vigorous. The arching branches can collect trash, and Dwarf Cutleaf Stephanandra should be placed where blowing trash is not a problem.

Propagation is by division, layering, root cuttings, and stem cuttings taken in July and August.

This plant is not seriously affected by insect pests or diseases.

Uses. Dwarf Cutleaf Stephanandra can be used to cover large or small areas on level ground or as an erosion control on slopes.

Stephanandra incisa 'Crispa' originated in a Danish nursery during the late 1930's.

Symphoricarpos orbiculatus

Indiancurrant Coralberry

Zone 3

Caprifoliaceae (Honeysuckle family)

Also known as Buckbrush, Coralberry, Indian Currant, Turkeyberry

May be listed as *Symphoricarpos vulgaris*

For color illustrations of *Symphoricarpos albus* and *Symphoricarpos × chenaultii,* see page 61.

stems, leaves, and fruits

Indiancurrant Coralberry is a dense, suckering, irregular, deciduous ground cover that grows 2 to 6 feet high and spreads 4 to 8 feet wide. The slender branches grow erect, and then arch to the ground. Growth rate is rapid. Texture is medium-fine in leaf, becoming coarser after the leaves have dropped.

Leaves. The leaves are opposite, simple, and ½ to 1½ inches long, with an ⅛-inch leafstalk. The leaf is oval to almost rounded, with a pointed to blunt apex and a rounded base. The margin is entire. The underside of the leaf is hairy and somewhat bloomy. The leaves are dull gray to blue-green during the summer, turning bluish gray to green in the fall. They persist on the plant late into the fall.

Stems. The slender stems are leafy. The young stems are pubescent; older stems have a grayish, papery bark. The pith is continuous.

Flowers. The bell-shaped flowers are ⅛ to ⅙ inch long, and range in color from greenish to yellowish white (sometimes tinged pink or purple). They are borne in dense axillary clusters or terminal spikes from July through August.

Fruits. The coral red to purplish, berrylike fruits are ⅙ to ¼ inch in diameter and ⅙ inch long, and are borne all along the stems. The fruits ripen in September and October, and persist on the plant into winter. They are used as food by wildlife.

Culture. Indiancurrant Coralberry grows well in full sun or partial sun on a wide variety of soils — acid or alkaline, poor or rich, drouthy or moist. It also tolerates city conditions.

Transplanting Indiancurrant Coralberry is not difficult. Container-grown plants or rooted suckers can be transplanted in the fall or spring. Space plants 2 to 4 feet apart. After the plant is established, pruning is usually the only cultural practice required. Prune in early spring before new growth begins. Indiancurrant Coralberry may eventually become weedy because of its suckering habit.

Propagation is by seeds, division, and softwood, semihardwood, and hardwood cuttings.

This plant is susceptible to attack by several insect pests and diseases, including anthracnose, berry rot, leafspot, powdery mildew, rusts, stem galls, aphids, snowberry clearwing, San Jose scale, and glacial white fly.

Uses. Indiancurrant Coralberry is most effective in naturalized areas. It can be used on slopes as an erosion control or on level ground, but may be too unkempt for use as a ground cover in small, refined areas.

Symphoricarpos orbiculatus is native from New Jersey to South Dakota and south to Texas and Georgia. It has escaped cultivation in New England and New York. This plant was introduced in 1727.

stems and fruits (winter)

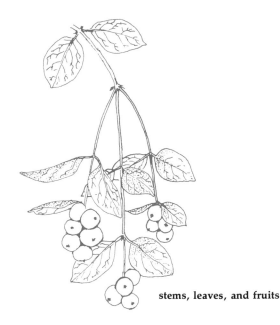

stems, leaves, and fruits

Symphoricarpos × chenaultii (Chenault Coralberry), which is closely related to Indiancurrant Coralberry, grows 3 to 4 feet high and spreads to 4 feet wide. Its growth habit is rounded-arching, and it is a somewhat "neater" plant than the Indiancurrant Coralberry. Growth rate is fast. Texture is fine.

The leaves are similar to those of Indiancurrant Coralberry except that they are smaller (½ to 1 inch long) and a dull, medium green. The pink flowers are borne in midsummer, and are clustered along the stems and in terminal spikes. The fruits are ¼ inch in diameter. They are reddish pink on the side facing the sun and whitish on the opposite side, although each side can be spotted with the other color. The fruits are borne in clusters along the stem and at its apex and persist until fall.

Chenault Coralberry grows best in full sun or partial shade on a well-drained, fertile soil. Space plants 2 to 4 feet apart.

Symphoricarpos × chenaultii originated about 1910 from a cross between *Symphoricarpos orbiculatus* and *Symphoricarpos microphyllus*. It is hardy in Zone 4.

Symphoricarpos × chenaultii 'Hancock' (Hancock Chenault Coralberry) is an excellent cultivar of Chenault Coralberry with similar flowers and fruits. It grows 2 feet high, and may spread to 10 feet wide. Growth rate is fast. The leaves are small and fine-textured. The stems may creep along the ground, rooting wherever they touch soil. This plant suckers readily, and grows well in many soils and locations. It originated in a Canadian nursery about 1940.

Symphoricarpos albus (Snowberry or Waxberry) is a twiggy, upright, deciduous shrub that grows 3 to 6 feet high and spreads 3 to 6 feet wide. The blue-green leaves are round to long oval, 1 to 2 inches long, and are not ornamentally colored in the fall. The small, inconspicuous, pinkish flowers are borne in terminal clusters from June through September. The snow-white fruits are ¼ to ⅝ inch wide, and are quite attractive in the landscape, especially when used with the red-fruited coralberries. They are produced from September through November. When Snowberry is heavy with fruits, the stems bend over, exposing the silvery green undersides of the leaves and giving the plant a completely altered appearance.

The best cultivars of *Symphoricarpos albus* for landscape use are 'Mother of Pearl' and 'White Hedge'.

Teucrium chamaedrys

Germander

Zone 5

Labiatae or Lamiaceae (Mint family)

Also known as Chamaedrys Germander

May be listed as *Teucrium pseudo-chamaedrys*

For a color illustration of *Teucrium chamaedrys,* see page 62.

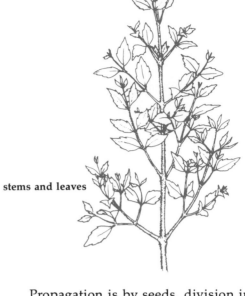

stems and leaves

Germander is a neat, dense, rounded ground cover that is evergreen in warm areas and deciduous in cool areas. It grows 8 to 18 inches high and spreads to 12 inches wide. The pubescent stems spread underground, and ascend at their ends. Growth rate is medium. Texture is medium-fine.

Leaves. The pubescent, lustrous, medium-green leaves are opposite, simple, and ¼ to 1 inch long, with a short leafstalk. The leaf is egg-shaped (with a pointed apex and a broadly wedge-shaped base). The margins of the main leaves are toothed; the floral leaves are entire. The leaves are slightly aromatic.

Flowers. The purple to rose-pink flowers are spotted with red and white, and have petals up to ⅗ inch long. They are borne in loose, upright terminal or axillary clusters of 2 to 6 flowers from June through September.

Fruits. The fruits are not ornamental.

Culture. Germander grows well in dry, well-drained soil. Deep, heavy roots allow the plant to bind the soil and tolerate drouth.

This plant grows best in full sun, but will also grow in light shade.

Germander can be transplanted from container-grown plants. Crowns and divisions should be planted in the spring. Plant crowns 1 inch deep. All plants should be spaced 8 to 15 inches apart. After the plants are established, apply mulch for winter protection. A hard winter can cause stem dieback. Dead branches should be pruned in early spring. Shearing Germander in the spring results in a denser plant. Recovery from shearing is usually rapid.

Propagation is by seeds, division in early spring, and stem cuttings taken in early summer.

This plant is not seriously affected by insect pests or diseases.

Uses. Germander can be used effectively in small, refined areas and rock gardens and on slight slopes. Because this plant recovers quickly from shearing, it is especially suitable for use as a low hedge or border.

leaves and flowers

Teucrium chamaedrys is native to southern and central Europe and western Asia. It was introduced in 1750.

*Thymus serpyllum**

Creeping Thyme
Zone 4

Labiatae or Lamiaceae (Mint family)

Also known as Mother-of-Thyme

May be listed as *Thymus angustifolius*

For color illustrations of *Thymus pseudolanuginosis* and *Thymus serpyllum* 'Coccineus', see page 62.

stems, leaves, and flowers

Creeping Thyme is a creeping, nearly herbaceous, ground-hugging, mat-forming, semievergreen ground cover that grows 1 to 3 inches high and spreads widely. The branches root as they creep, and the ends of the branches ascend. Growth rate is slow. Texture is fine.

Leaves. The soft, medium-green leaves are opposite, simple, and ⅕ to ½ inch long, with a short leafstalk. The leaf is narrowly oval, with a rounded apex and a broadly wedge-shaped base. The margins are entire. The lower leaf surface may be hairless to slightly hairy, and both the upper and lower surfaces may be dotted with resin. The leaves are aromatic.

Flowers. The narrow, fragrant, attractive, bell-shaped flowers are dark-pink to reddish purple, ¼ inch long, and hairy at the base. They are borne in upright clusters at the ends of the stems from June through September.

Culture. Creeping Thyme grows best in hot, dry, poor, slightly alkaline, well-drained soils, but will tolerate soils with a pH of 6.5 to 7.5. This plant is drouth-resistant, and can grow on slightly sloping sites. Although full sun is preferable, Creeping Thyme will grow in light shade.

Container-grown plants, clumps of plants, or rooted stems can be transplanted. Transplant in the spring. Space plants ½ to 1½ feet apart. After the plants are established, Creeping Thyme requires little care. Fertilization is usually not necessary. In fact, the plants become taller, weaker, and less attractive if grown in rich or extremely fertile soils. Pull or hoe out unwanted plants. To keep the planting neat, trim in early spring before the flowers bloom.

Propagation is by seeds, division, and cuttings.

This plant is susceptible to attack by root rot and mealy bugs.

Uses. Creeping Thyme should be planted in highly visible sites. It tolerates occasional foot traffic, and grows well between stepping-stones or along walkways. The plants release a pleasant aroma when bruised.

Thymus serpyllum is native to central and southern Europe, Asia Minor, and the north and central portions of the Balkan peninsula.

A great many selections of *Thymus serpyllum* are available. One common selection is Wooly-Mother-of-Thyme, which has long been sold as *Thymus serpyllum* 'Lanuginosus' or *Thymus lanuginosus*. The correct botanical name is *Thymus pseudolanuginosis*. It is a low, creeping plant with oval leaves that are hairy on both sides, giving it a gray appearance. The flowers are a pale pink. Another widely sold selection is 'Coccineus'. The plants sold as 'Coccineus' have reddish flowers, and may be selections of *Thymus praecox*, *Thymus serpyllum*, or *Thymus vulgaris*.

---

* According to *Hortus III*, *Thymus serpyllum* is rarely cultivated in the United States, and most of the plants sold under that name are actually *Thymus nummularius*, *Thymus pannonicus*, *Thymus praecox*, *Thymus pseudolanuginosus*, or *Thymus pulegioides*. This explanation may partially account for the wide variation among plants listed as *Thymus serpyllum*.

Vinca minor

Common Periwinkle

Zone 4

Apocynaceae (Dogbane family)

Also known as Creeping Myrtle, Dwarf Periwinkle, Lesser Periwinkle, Myrtle, Periwinkle, Running Myrtle, Small Periwinkle

For color illustrations of *Vinca minor* and *Vinca minor* 'Alba', see page 62.

stems, leaves, and flowers

Common Periwinkle is a trailing, mat-forming, vinelike, evergreen ground cover that grows 6 inches high and spreads widely. The branches root as they creep. Growth rate is medium to fast (fast if the plant is placed on the proper site). Texture is medium-fine.

Leaves. The leaves are opposite, simple, entire, and ¾ to 1⅗ inches long, with a short leafstalk. They are oval, with a rounded-to-pointed apex and a base that tapers into the leafstalk, hairless, glossy, and dark green above and paler green beneath. When broken, the leafstalk may exude a milky juice.

Flowers. The funnel-shaped, perfect, lilac-blue flowers are solitary, and have 5 petals with spreading lobes. The flowers are stalked and about 1 inch wide. They are borne mainly in April, but appear sporadically until late summer.

Fruits. The fruits are follicles about 3 inches long, and are not ornamental.

Culture. Common Periwinkle grows best in a moist, fertile, organic soil with a pH of 4.5 to 7.5. It will tolerate poorer soils, but growth is slowed. Do not plant in wet sites.

Common Periwinkle tolerates full sun to fairly heavy shade. When grown in full sun, the leaves may be less glossy and lighter green. Protection from winter winds and sun is necessary.

Bare-root plants, clumps, or container-grown plants can be transplanted. Transplant in the spring, and space plants 6 to 14 inches apart. Plants placed 12 inches apart may require 1 to 2 years to cover. An organic mulch aids in establishment. At planting time, cut back bare-root plants and clumps to compensate for root loss. All plants should be pinched to cause branching, resulting in a denser cover.

It may be necessary to irrigate during hot,

dry periods. The plants benefit from an application of a complete, balanced fertilizer and shearing each spring. Do not use high-nitrogen fertilizers. Shearing causes the plants to branch and maintain their vigor. Weeds are rarely a problem because of the cover's denseness.

Propagation is by division in the spring, root cuttings, sod, and stem cuttings in the summer.

This plant is susceptible to several diseases, including canker and dieback, blight leaf spot, and root rot. Do not plant in areas with poor air movement and water drainage. Ask your county Extension adviser for control recommendations.

Uses. Common Periwinkle can be grown on slight slopes and on level ground, and in large or small areas. It is especially attractive beneath trees and shrubs.

Vinca minor is native to Europe and western Asia, and has escaped cultivation in the United States. It has been cultivated since ancient times.

Many selections of *Vinca minor* are available. The flowers can be single or double, and may range in color from white to blue to purple. Popular selections include 'Alba', 'Bowles', and 'Variegata'. 'Alba' is less vigorous than the species, and has white flowers and lighter green leaves. It blooms sporadically all summer. 'Bowles' has a clumping rather than a trailing habit. It is vigorous, and has showier, darker blue flowers and larger leaves than the species. 'Variegata' has blue flowers with gold variegated leaves, and may require more sun than the species.

Xanthorhiza simplicissima

Yellowroot

Zone 4

Ranunculaceae (Buttercup family)

Also known as Shrub Yellowroot

May be listed as *Xanthorhiza apiifolia,*
Zanthorhiza apiifolia

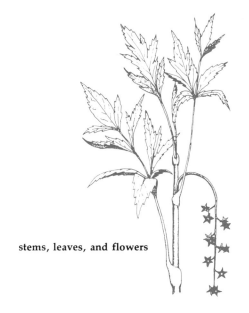

stems, leaves, and flowers

Yellowroot is a suckering, uniform, deciduous ground cover that grows 1 to 3 feet high and spreads freely. The stems are erect, and are usually sparsely branched. Growth rate is medium. Texture is medium.

Leaves. The long-stalked leaves are alternate, pinnately or bipinnately compound, and commonly occur in dense clusters at the tops of the stems. The egg-shaped to oval leaflets (generally 5 per leaf) vary from 1 to 3 inches in length. The margins of the leaflets can be toothed or have various serrations. During the summer, the leaflets are yellow-green to bright green, turning to yellow, golden, or orange in the fall. The overall appearance of the leaf is celerylike.

Stems. The branchlets are a pale greenish gray. The older stems are usually single, brownish yellow, and have a large, continuous pith. The leaf scars are slightly curved, and encircle more than one-half the stem. The inner bark and the roots are yellow.

Flowers. The star-shaped, brownish purple flowers are perfect, less than ¼ inch wide, 5-petaled, and usually inconspicuous. They are borne in 2- to 3-inch, drooping clusters in the leaf base from late April through early May.

Fruits. The fruits are 1-seeded, dehiscent follicles that are not ornamental.

Culture. Yellowroot grows best in moist soils, and often occurs in low areas near ponds or streams. It tolerates being submerged, and can be used to control weeds near water. This plant will grow, however, in a wide variety of soils, even heavy soils. If grown in dryer soils, it spreads less vigorously.

Yellowroot will grow in full sun to partial shade and beneath trees.

Transplant in the spring or fall. Space plants 1½ to 2 feet apart. Divisions should be made in the spring. After the plant has become established, little care is necessary. It will spread rapidly, and may soon get out of control in small areas. If pruning is required, prune in late winter before new growth starts.

Propagation is by seeds, division in the spring, and root cuttings taken in the fall.

This plant is not seriously affected by insect pests or diseases.

Uses. Yellowroot can be used near the edges of ponds, streams, or other low areas, as well as on banks or beneath trees. This plant may be too high for small, refined gardens.

Xanthorhiza simplicissima is native to the eastern United States, from New York to Kentucky and southward. It was introduced in 1776.

Arctostaphylos uva-ursi
Bearberry
page 15

Cotoneaster horizontalis
Rockspray Cotoneaster
page 21

Comptonia peregrina
Sweetfern
page 16

Cotoneaster horizontalis (fruits)
Rockspray Cotoneaster
page 21

Cornus canadensis (flowers)
Bunchberry
page 17

Cytisus decumbens
Prostrate Broom
page 22

Euonymus fortunei 'Colorata'
Purple Wintercreeper
page 24

Forsythia viridissima 'Bronxensis' (foliage)
Bronx Greenstem Forsythia
page 27

Euonymus fortunei 'Silver Queen'
page 26

Forsythia viridissima 'Bronxensis' (flowers)
Bronx Greenstem Forsythia
page 27

Hedera helix
English Ivy
page 28

Juniperus chinensis var. *procumbens* 'Nana'
Dwarf Japgarden Juniper
page 30

Juniperus horizontalis 'Plumosa'
Andorra Creeping Juniper
page 34

Juniperus conferta
Shore Juniper
page 32

Juniperus horizontalis 'Wiltonii'
Blue Rug Creeping Juniper
page 35

Lonicera alpigena 'Nana'
Dwarf Alps Honeysuckle
page 40

Mahonia repens
Creeping Mahonia
page 41

Lonicera japonica 'Aureo-reticulata'
Yellownet Honeysuckle
page 40

Mitchella repens
Partridgeberry
page 42

Lonicera sempervirens
Trumpet Honeysuckle
page 40

Pachysandra terminalis 'Green Carpet'
page 43

Symphoricarpos albus
Snowberry
page 51

Rhus aromatica 'Gro-Low' (fruits)
Gro-Low Fragrant Sumac
page 45

Symphoricarpos × chenaultii (fruits)
Chenault Coralberry
page 51

Salix repens 'Nitida'
page 47

Teucrium chamaedrys
Germander
page 52

Thymus pseudolanuginosis
Wooly-Mother-of-Thyme
page 53

Vinca minor
Common Periwinkle
page 54

Thymus serpyllum 'Coccineus'
page 53

Vinca minor 'Alba'
White Periwinkle
page 54

Achillea millefolium
Common Yarrow
page 75

Achillea millefolium var. *rosea*
page 75

Aegopodium podagraria (Goutweed), right;
Aegopodium podagraria 'Variegatum'
(Silveredge Goutweed), left.
page 77

Ajuga pyramidalis 'Metallica Crispa'
page 79

Alchemilla vulgaris
Lady's-Mantle
page 80

Arabis caucasica
Rockcress
page 81

Arenaria verna
Moss Sandwort
page 83

Asarum europaeum
European Evergreen Ginger
page 85

Asarum canadense
Wild Ginger
page 84

Brunnera macrophylla
Hardy Forget-me-not
page 86

Cerastium tomentosum
Snow-in-Summer
page 88

Coronilla varia
Crown Vetch
page 92

Ceratostigma plumbaginoides
Leadwort
page 89

Coronilla varia (flowers)
Crown Vetch
page 92

Epimedium species
Barrenwort
page 94

Epimedium × *rubrum*
Red Epimedium
page 97

Filipendula vulgaris 'Flore Pleno'
page 100

Festuca ovina var. *glauca*
Blue Fescue
page 99

Galium odoratum
Sweet Woodruff
page 101

Filipendula vulgaris
Dropwort
page 100

Geranium species
Cranesbill
page 102

Hemerocallis fulva
Tawny Daylily
page 109

Geranium ibericum 'Album'

page 105

Hemerocallis fulva (flowers)
Tawny Daylily
page 109

Geranium sanguineum
Bloodred Geranium
page 106

Hemerocallis hybrid
page 110

Hosta sieboldii
Seersucker Plantain-Lily
page 117

Iberis sempervirens 'Snowflake'
page 119

Hosta lancifolia
Narrow-leaved Plantain-Lily
page 115

Lamiastrum galeobdolon 'Variegatum' (leaves)
Yellow Archangel
page 121

Lathyrus latifolius
Perennial Pea
page 123

Pachysandra procumbens (spring growth)
Allegany Pachysandra
page 128

Liriope spicata
Lilyturf
page 124

Phlox subulata
Moss Pink
page 130

Nepeta × *faassenii*
Catmint
page 127

Phalaris arundinacea var. *picta*
Ribbon Grass
page 129

Potentilla tabernaemontani
Potentilla verna
page 134

Polygonum bistorta
Snakeweed
page 133

Pulmonaria officinalis
Jerusalem Cowslip
page 136

Polygonum cuspidatum var. *compactum*
Low Japanese Fleeceflower
page 132

Ranunculus repens
Creeping Buttercup
page 137

Sedum spurium 'Dragon's Blood'
page 146

Saponaria ocymoides
Rock Soapwort
page 138

Sempervivum species (collection)
Houseleek
page 147

Sedum acre 'Minus'
page 141

Sempervivum arachnoideum
var. *tomentosum*
page 149

Veronica repens
Creeping Speedwell
page 154

Verbena canadensis
Rose Verbena
page 150

Veronica incana
Woolly Speedwell
page 152

Waldsteinia ternata
Barren Strawberry
page 155

Herbaceous
Ground Covers

Typical Entry

Galium odoratum .... botanical name

Sweet Woodruff .... most often used common name

Zone 4 .... hardiness zone

Rubiaceae (Madder family) .... family name

Also known as Sweet Woodroof, Woodruff .... other common names

May be listed as *Asperula odorata* .... obsolete botanical name

Achillea millefolium

Common Yarrow

Zone 3

Asteraceae or Compositae (Sunflower family)

Also known as Milfoil

For color illustrations of *Achillea millefolium* and *Achillea millifolium* var. *rosea*, see page 63.

Common Yarrow is seldom cultivated in the United States (see recommended selections below). It is a weedy, deciduous ground cover that spreads rapidly by rhizomes. Each plant is composed of a basal rosette of leaves from which a leafy, flowering stalk arises in the summer. The leafy rosettes form loose mats about 4 inches high; the flower stalks grow 2½ to 3 feet high. Texture is very fine.

Leaves. The aromatic leaves are divided into innumerable fine leaflets, and appear soft and fernlike. The rosette leaves are long-petioled and much longer than they are wide. They are broadest toward the apex, and gradually taper to the base. The stem leaves are alternate, without a petiole, and linear (narrow with parallel sides). The leaves and stems are usually covered with soft, whitish hairs but may be almost hairless.

Flowers. What appear to be individual flowers are actually the tight heads of very small flowers (each head is about ½ inch wide). The ray flowers that surround each head are showy, white, and petallike. The heads are clustered in round or flat-topped corymbs 2 to 3 inches wide. Flowering begins in June and continues throughout most of the summer. Removing the old, faded flower clusters will extend flowering well into September.

Culture. Common Yarrow grows best in full sun in a dry, well-drained soil with average to low fertility. Flowering is usually inferior in moist, rich soils. Mowing Common Yarrow 2 to 3 times during the growing season will keep it low growing and result in a faster spread. If the plants are not mowed, they should be cut back after flowering.

Common Yarrow may be planted at any time from early spring to early fall. Space plants 1 to 2 feet apart. Applying a fertilizer that is low in nitrogen and high in phosphorus and potassium (such as 5-10-10) to the planting bed will aid in establishment. Continued fertilization is not recommended; overcrowding and other problems may develop.

Propagation is by seeds, division in the spring, and stem cuttings taken in the summer.

This plant is generally free from insect pests and diseases. Powdery mildew and stem rot may occur on sites that are too moist or during extended periods of wet weather.

Uses. Common Yarrow will grow on almost any sunny, well-drained site. It is an excellent plant for colonizing areas with poor, dry soil where grass will not grow.

Achillea millefolium is native to Europe and western Asia, and has become widely naturalized in North America. The genus name *Achillea* honors the Greek hero Achilles, who is said to have used this plant to heal wounds during the Trojan War.

Recommended selections of *Achillea millefolium* are the variety *rosea* and the cultivars 'Crimson Beauty', 'Fire King', 'Kelwayi', and 'Red Beauty'. The variety *rosea* has bright pink ray flowers that become faded as they age, and the cultivars have deeper colored ray flowers ranging from rosy pink to red. All of these selections are less vigorous than the species (do not spread as rapidly), have more attractive and longer blooming flowers, and are lower growing (1½ to 2 feet high).

Achillea tomentosa

Woolly Yarrow

Zone 2

Asteraceae or Compositae (Sunflower family)

Woolly Yarrow is closely related to *Achillea millefolium*. It is generally considered a better ground cover because of its lower height and dense basal leaves that form tight mats.

Leaves. Like the other yarrows, Woolly Yarrow has very finely cut, fernlike leaves that are aromatic when crushed. The leaves and stems are densely woolly, with long, silvery hairs. The foliage forms tight mats of basal rosettes up to 4 inches high.

Flowers. The flower heads are about 1 foot high on leafy stalks; their conspicuous, bright yellow ray flowers occur from June to September.

Culture. Woolly Yarrow is drouth tolerant, and can be grown in almost any well-drained soil. It grows best in full sun, but will grow in partial shade. This plant spreads rapidly by surface runners in all but the poorest soils. In rich soils, Woolly Yarrow may quickly become overcrowded, requiring annual thinning.

Removing the faded flower heads will enhance and prolong flowering. To rejuvenate the foliage and create more compact mats, mow or cut back the plants after they have flowered. Mowing Woolly Yarrow 2 to 3 times during the growing season will keep it about 4 inches high and prevent flowering.

Plant in early spring or fall. Space plants ½ to 1 foot apart in poor soils or to obtain rapid cover and 1 to 2 feet apart in soils with average or better-than-average fertility.

Propagation is by rooted runners (which can be easily separated from the plant and transplanted in early spring), and by stem cuttings taken in the summer.

Uses. Woolly Yarrow is an excellent ground cover for hot, dry sites with full sun. It is especially useful in areas with infertile soil where it can be easily contained. When mowed regularly, Woolly Yarrow is an attractive lawn substitute in areas with little foot traffic. This plant is often used in rock gardens and between paving stones. Its vivid yellow flowers and leaves that remain green late in the year are ornamental assets.

Achillea tomentosa is native to Europe and western Asia.

A recommended selection is *Achillea tomentosa* 'Moonlight'. This plant has pale yellow ray flowers, and is somewhat less vigorous than the species.

Aegopodium podagraria

Goutweed

Zone 3

Apiaceae or Umbelliferae (Carrot family)

Also known as Ashweed, Bishop's Weed, Ground Ash, Ground Elder, Herb Gerard

For a color illustration of *Aegopodium podagraria* and *Aegopodium podagraria* 'Variegatum', see page 63.

Goutweed is a persistent, weedy ground cover that forms a foliage mass to about 1 foot high. It spreads rapidly by rhizomes, and dies to the ground with the first hard freeze in the autumn. Texture is medium.

Leaves. The leaves are compound, with petioles that are expanded at the base and encircle the stem. The leaflets are arranged in 3 groups of 3 leaflets each (biternate), and are coarsely serrate. They are broad at the base and narrow to a sharp point at the apex.

Flowers. The small, white flowers are borne in compound umbels in June on leafy stems 1½ to 2 feet high. The overall effect is not ornamentally significant.

Culture. Goutweed grows well in almost any soil, and tolerates both wet and dry conditions. It is a very hardy, vigorous plant, and is adaptable to the full range of light (from full sun to deep shade).

This plant is easy to grow. In average soil under normal conditions, plants spaced 1 foot apart will fill in after 1 to 2 growing seasons. Goutweed is easily transplanted in either the spring or fall. Once established, it is highly competitive and deeply rooted, requiring no feeding and water except during periods of extreme weather. Mowing or clipping the planting to a height of 6 inches 2 to 3 times a season will eliminate the flowers and seeds and keep it low and compact. The seeds germinate readily, and may become a nuisance in the lawn.

Goutweed is most easily propagated by division in early spring and early fall.

This plant is not seriously affected by insect pests or diseases.

Uses. Goutweed should be used in poor soil areas where little else will grow, or where it can be easily contained (such as between a sidewalk and a building). It is a good choice for areas of deep shade because it competes well with trees for soil nutrients and moisture.

Aegopodium podagraria is native to Europe, and has become naturalized in North America. One of its common names, Bishop's Weed, is said to have arisen from the belief that this plant's persistence in the garden would cause even a bishop to swear.

A recommended selection is *Aegopodium podagraria* 'Variegatum' (Silveredge Goutweed, Silveredge Bishop's Weed). Because Silveredge Goutweed is somewhat less vigorous and its variegated foliage more attractive in the landscape than the species, it is a more desirable ornamental. Its foliage, which is light green irregularly edged with white, serves to brighten areas of deep shade where grass will not grow. Although this plant grows well in full sun, the foliage is likely to scorch.

Ajuga reptans

Bugleweed

Zone 4

Lamiaceae or Labiatae (Mint family)

Also known as Bugle, Carpet Bugle

For a color illustration of *Ajuga pyramidalis* 'Metallica Crispa', see page 63.

Bugleweed is a semievergreen to evergreen ground cover that forms dense mats 4 to 6 inches high. The ground-hugging rosettes of glossy leaves spread quickly by stolons. The leafy flower stalks that arise from the rosettes grow to 1 foot high. Texture is coarse.

Leaves. The lustrous dark-green leaves are opposite, and are borne in flat, basal rosettes on square stems. The rosette and stolon leaves are 2½ to 3 inches long and 1 inch wide. They are narrowly oblong to elliptic, and entire or repand (with a wavy margin). The leaf base narrows to form a short petiole. The stem leaves are smaller and very short petioled or without a petiole (sessile). The species and its green-foliage forms turn bronze to reddish with the first frost in the autumn.

Flowers. The violet-blue to purple (rarely white or red) flowers are arranged in crowded axillary whorls on erect, leafy stems. The lower whorls of flowers are distant on the stem; the upper ones are borne close together. The flowers are asymmetrical, with a 2-lipped corolla (the upper lip is small and weakly 2-lobed, and the lower lip is 3-lobed and spreading). Flowering occurs from May through June, and is most prolific in full sun.

Culture. Bugleweed spreads rapidly by stolons, forming a tight cover that virtually eliminates weeds. This plant will grow in full sun to heavy shade, although it may not flower well in dense shade. Nearly any moist, well-drained soil is suitable. Bugleweed is shallow rooted, and should be watered during periods of drouth. Fertilize twice during the growing season for

best growth. Water the planting immediately after application to remove fertilizer from the leaves; otherwise, the foliage may be burned.

Flowering stems may be cut back or the planting mowed lightly after the blooms have faded. The species may seed itself, but cultivars will not reproduce true from seeds. These seedlings must be weeded out when they appear.

Bugleweed is semievergreen to deciduous in colder climates, and is subject to winter kill in open, exposed locations. It should be planted where it is protected from winter winds. A loose mulch is also helpful.

Plant Bugleweed in the spring. Space plants 1 foot apart. For better moisture retention, add peat moss or well-rotted organic matter to the planting bed. Apply a low-nitrogen fertilizer such as 5-10-10 to promote strong root growth.

Propagation is by seeds or division of rooted plantlets from stolons in the spring or fall.

This plant is susceptible to crown rot, root nematodes, and certain fungal diseases. Planting in a well-drained soil and thinning the plants to prevent overcrowding will reduce these problems. Bugleweed may invade surrounding lawn areas, but can be controlled with a broadleaf weed killer. Ask your county Extension adviser for recommendations.

Uses. Bugleweed provides quick cover. A single plant sends out stolons in all directions that root at the nodes, resulting in new plantlets that cover a 3-foot-square area in a single growing season. This plant is used most effectively in irrigated beds and in dense shade where grass will not grow. It makes an excellent ground cover under deciduous shade trees as long as it receives supplemental fertilizer and moisture. The crisp, glossy leaves are quite handsome, and the numerous cultivars offer a wide variety of foliage color choices.

Ajuga reptans is native to Europe.

Ajuga reptans hybridizes readily with *Ajuga genevensis* and *Ajuga pyramidalis*, resulting in many different forms. There are also numerous cultivars of these species, particularly *Ajuga reptans*, that are available commercially. The nomenclature of the cultivars and hybrids is often confusing. You should read the plant description carefully and, if possible, see an actual plant before making a purchase.

Selected cultivars of *Ajuga reptans* include the following: 'Alba' (creamy white flowers); 'Burgundy Glow' (the tricolored foliage is green, creamy white, and dark pink); 'Giant Bronze' (somewhat larger than the species and a metallic bronze color); 'Jungle Green' (the leaves are crisped, green, and larger and more rounded than the species); 'Multicoloris' (the green leaves are mottled red, white, and yellow); 'Purpurea' (the foliage is medium to dark purple and the flowers are dark purple); 'Rosea' (the flowers are rose pink); 'Tottenhamii' (the leaves turn bronzish purple in the fall and the flowers are purple); and 'Variegata' (a less vigorous form with leaves that are mottled creamy white and that scorch easily when grown in full sun).

Ajuga pyramidalis 'Metallica Crispa' is usually more readily available than the *Ajuga reptans* cultivars. This attractive, vigorous form has crisp, bronzish purple leaves with a metallic sheen. The leaves are tinted red in the autumn. The flowers are deep blue. The species *Ajuga pyramidalis* is a rhizomatous, clump-forming perennial. It is easily propagated by division of clumps in the spring.

Ajuga genevensis is a related species that is not as desirable a ground cover as *Ajuga reptans* or *Ajuga pyramidalis* 'Metallica Crispa'. It is an erect, clump-forming perennial that grows 4 to 16 inches high, and spreads slowly by short rhizomes. The leaves and stems are hairy to almost glabrous (smooth); the violet flowers are borne in May and June in many-flowered axillary whorls. This plant is not quite as hardy as *Ajuga reptans,* and is subject to winter kill. In addition, the plants require closer spacing for adequate coverage. Propagation is by clump division in the spring.

Alchemilla vulgaris

Lady's-Mantle

Zone 4

Rosaceae (Rose family)

Also known as Common Lady's-Mantle

May be listed as *Alchemilla mollis*

For a color illustration of *Alchemilla vulgaris*, see see page 63.

Lady's-Mantle is a deciduous, clump-forming ground cover that grows to 1½ feet high and spreads by means of creeping rootstocks. Growth rate is slow to medium. Texture is coarse.

Leaves. Most of the soft, hairy to almost glabrous (smooth), grayish green leaves arise directly from the roots. The leaves are large (up to 6 inches wide) and broadly rounded, with a shallow incurve where the petiole is attached. They are folded lengthwise like a fan (plicate) and shallowly lobed, with 7 to 11 toothed lobes.

Flowers. The small, yellow-green, apetalous (without petals) flowers are produced in compound cymes above the foliage mass. Lady's-Mantle blooms from May through June. The flower clusters are not showy.

Culture. Lady's-Mantle requires little care, and is easily grown in almost any ordinary garden soil that has been supplemented with organic matter. This plant grows best in sites with light to medium shade. It tends to seed itself generously, and old flower clusters should be removed before they produce seed.

Before new growth starts in early spring, cut back and remove the old foliage remaining from the previous growing season. Apply a well-rotted organic mulch in the spring.

Plant in the spring. Space plants 1½ feet apart.

Propagation is by seeds and clump division in the spring.

Lady's-Mantle is not seriously affected by insect pests or diseases.

Uses. This plant has traditionally been used in the perennial border. When massed, the clumps of handsome, pleated foliage make an attractive ground cover with an interesting texture.

Alchemilla vulgaris is native to the northern temperate regions of the Old World.

Arabis caucasica

Rockcress

Zone 3

Brassicaceae or Cruciferae (Mustard family)

Also known as Wall Cress, Wall Rockcress

May be listed as *Arabis albida*

For a color illustration of *Arabis caucasica*, see page 64.

Rockcress is a vigorous, sturdy ground cover with foliage that remains late in the season, often persisting throughout the winter. Its spreading or trailing stems form mats of foliage 3 to 4 inches high and 18 inches wide. The flowers are borne in loose clusters above the foliage on stems 6 to 8 inches high. Growth rate is medium to rapid. Texture is fine.

Leaves. The nearly evergreen leaves are 1 to 3 inches long, and are covered with a whitish pubescence. They are tufted in basal rosettes or borne alternately on prostrate stems. The tufted basal leaves are usually egg-shaped, with the wider end toward the apex and the narrow end tapering to the base. The stem leaves have extended, rounded (auriculate) or pointed (sagittate) basal lobes. The leaves may be entire (without lobes or teeth) or slightly lobed or coarsely toothed toward the apex.

Flowers. The fragrant, symmetrical, white flowers are complete, with 4 showy petals that are ½ inch long. They are borne profusely from April to early May in loose racemes on 6- to 8-inch stems.

Culture. Rockcress grows best in a sandy or gravelly, slightly alkaline soil in full sun or light shade. It will, however, tolerate almost any well-drained soil. Prolonged wet weather can result in mediocre flowering, and soggy soils may cause downy mildew and clubroot.

Rockcress should be severely cut back (about halfway to the ground) after flowering. Shearing or pruning the plants prevents their becoming sprawling and unkempt and encourages branching and a more compact habit.

If Rockcress is planted in a well-drained soil, it requires little care. Space plants 6 to 9 inches apart in the early spring. Add well-rotted organic matter or bonemeal to the planting bed. Do not apply a fast-acting fertilizer. A soil that is too fertile can damage the plants. Apply compost or bonemeal lightly every second or third growing season to keep the planting vigorous. Rockcress can be transplanted while in flower as long as the roots are accompanied by a ball of soil.

This plant is deciduous in colder climates where there is no continuous snow cover, and is subject to winter burn and damage in open locations. A light covering of evergreen boughs applied after the ground has frozen is beneficial.

Propagation is by seeds, softwood cuttings, and division in the spirng. Softwood cuttings of new growth taken immediately after flowering will root readily.

Uses. Rockcress has traditionally been used in rock gardens and on top of retaining walls. As a ground cover, it is best used in small, sandy or gravelly areas in full sun where it is also protected from harsh winter winds. When grown adjacent to less vigorous, more delicate plants, its spread may need to be contained. Rockcress is valued for its soft, grayish foliage and long life.

Arabis caucasica is native to the Caucasus Mountains.

Recommended selections of *Arabis caucasica* are 'Flore Pleno', a double-flowering form, and 'Spring Charm'. 'Flore Pleno' is preferable to the species because it has much showier flowers that last for a longer period of time. 'Spring Charm' produces rosy pink flowers. There is also a variegated foliage form (the leaves are margined with creamy white), but this plant tends to revert to the normal foliage coloration of the species.

Arabis caucasica is easily confused with *Arabis alpina* (Alpine Rockcress). Alpine Rockcress may be distinguished from Rockcress by its slightly less pubescent leaves, its smaller, more compact growth habit, and its shorter flower petals (3/8 inch long). The two plants have the same cultural requirements and uses.

Another closely related species is *Arabis procurrens* (may be listed as *Arabis mollis*). This plant is easily distinguished by its stoloniferous growth habit and its glossy, dark-green leaves that are slightly pubescent only on the margins and undersides. The foliage forms tufted mats that are only 1 to 2 inches high. The flowers rise above the foliage on leafy stems 10 to 12 inches high. The cultural requirements and uses of *Arabis procurrens* are identical with those of *Arabis caucasica* and *Arabis alpina*.

Arenaria verna

Moss Sandwort

Zone 2

Caryophyllaceae (Pink family)

Also known as Irish Moss

May be listed as *Arenaria caespitosa, Arenaria verna caespitosa, Minuartia verna*

For a color illustration of *Arenaria verna*, see page 64.

Moss Sandwort is a mat-forming, mosslike, evergreen ground cover that grows 1 to 6 inches high. The tiny flowers are borne in profusion about 1 inch above the foliage. Growth rate is medium to fast. Texture is very fine.

Leaves. The leaves are about ¾ inch long, very narrow with parallel sides, and taper to a sharp point at the apex. They are opposite, and produced on prostrate, sterile stems and sparingly on upright, often branching, flowering stems.

Flowers. The starlike, white flowers are borne in 2-flowered to many-flowered cymes on erect, leafy stems in May. Each flower has 5 petals and is ¼ inch wide.

Culture. Moss Sandwort grows best in a slightly acid, sandy loam, but will grow in almost any fertile, well-drained soil. Adding sand or peat moss to the planting bed is beneficial. This plant thrives in partial shade, but tolerates full sun if supplied with adequate moisture.

Although quite hardy, Moss Sandwort suffers winter damage in open, exposed locations in cold climates. (The foliage turns a silvery color when the plant is injured.)

In its native habitat, Moss Sandwort is covered with snow throughout the winter months. If snow cover is not continuous, apply a light mulch that does not pack down, such as straw, pine needles, evergreen boughs, etc. To prevent fungal diseases, remove this mulch before growth starts. Good drainage is also essential to winter survival because this plant will not tolerate slush. Winter shade will help prevent foliage discoloration.

Once established, Moss Sandwort is so dense that weeds do not invade it. After several growing seasons, the planting may have a lumpy or undulating appearance because of crowding. This problem can be alleviated by cutting and removing thin strips from the planting and then tamping down the plants remaining in the bed.

Moss Sandwort should be fertilized annually with a low-nitrogen fertilizer such as 5-10-10. The foliage will become brown during prolonged periods of hot, dry weather, but recovers quickly when watered. Because this plant is shallow-rooted, it should receive supplemental moisture whenever rainfall is sparse.

Plant in early spring. Space plants 6 inches apart. A well-prepared, fertilized bed will produce total coverage in 1 to 2 growing seasons.

The best method of propagation is by division in the early spring. Moss Sandwort may also be grown from seeds sown in the spring or from stem cuttings taken in early summer.

This plant is not seriously affected by insect pests of diseases.

Uses. Moss Sandwort is an excellent ground cover for relatively small areas. One of the best uses for this plant is on a gentle, sandy slope in partial shade. It is tolerant of foot traffic, and can be used effectively between stepping-stones or as a filler between flagstones or brick. It is valued for its carpeting, evergreen foliage, and tiny, starlike flowers.

Arenaria verna is native to alpine regions of the Northern Hemisphere.

Moss Sandwort is quite similar to *Sagina subulata* (Corsican Pearlwort), and is often confused with this plant. Moss Sandwort may be distinguished by its 3-veined leaves that are up to ¾ inch long. The leaves of Corsican Pearlwort are rarely more than ¼ inch long, and usually appear unveined. The cultural requirements and uses of these two closely related species are identical.

Arenaria verna 'Aurea' (Golden Moss Sandwort) is a yellow-green foliage form that is much less vigorous than the species.

Asarum canadense

Wild Ginger

Zone 3

Aristolochiaceae (Birthwort family)

Also known as Canada Snakeroot

For a color illustration of *Asarum canadense*, see page 64.

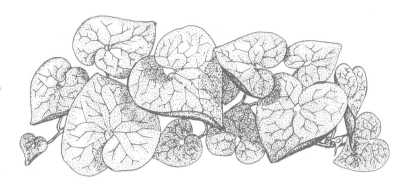

Wild Ginger is a deciduous ground cover that forms a foliage mass up to 6 inches high and spreads rapidly by rhizomes. It is somewhat hardier than European Evergreen Ginger (see page 85), and can be grown in a wider variety of locations. Texture is coarse.

Leaves. The large (5 to 6 inches wide), leathery, dark-green leaves are kidney-shaped, with deeply impressed veins. The leaves are paired, and arise from the rhizomes on petioles that may reach 12 inches in length. Both leaves and petioles are somewhat pubescent.

Flowers. The rich purplish or reddish brown flowers, hidden by the leaves, arise from the leaf axils. The pointed calyx lobes are up to ¾ inch long and spreading or reflexed (bent sharply back around the outside of the calyx). The flowers are produced in April and May and persist for several months.

Culture. The cultural requirements for Ginger are the same as those for European Evergreen Ginger (see page 85) except that winter protection is not required. Mulching may be beneficial in areas exposed to winter sun and wind.

Propagation is by division of the rhizomes in early spring before new growth starts.

Uses. Wild Ginger is an excellent ground cover for partially shaded to densely shaded sites.

Asarum canadense is native to rich woodlands from New Brunswick south to South Carolina and west to Missouri and Ontario.

Wild Ginger and European Evergreen Ginger are not related to the culinary ginger (*Zingiber officinale*) of tropical origin. Their names refer to the spicy fragrance of the freshly cut or crushed rhizomes and leaves. The American Indians and early settlers collected and dried the roots of Wild Ginger for use as a substitute for the culinary ginger.

Asarum europaeum

European Evergreen Ginger

Zone 4

Aristolochiaceae (Birthwort family)

Also known as Shiny-leaf Ginger

For a color illustration of *Asarum europaeum*, see page 64.

European Evergreen Ginger is an evergreen ground cover that grows 5 to 6 inches high and spreads by creeping surface rhizomes. Growth rate is slow. Texture is coarse.

Leaves. The glossy, leathery leaves arise in pairs directly from the nodes of the rhizomes. The leaf is heart-shaped to kidney-shaped, 2 to 3 inches wide, and is borne on a fleshy petiole up to 5 inches long.

Flowers. The unusual flowers of gingers are often unnoticed because they are borne near the soil surface under the foliage. They arise from the axils of the leafstalks, and are apetalous, with a cup-shaped calyx that is divided into 3 pointed lobes. The greenish purple or brown flowers of European Evergreen Ginger are ½ inch wide, and are borne singly in April and May.

Culture. This plant grows best in full shade to very dense shade, but will tolerate partial shade. It requires a moist, humus-rich soil with a pH from 5.5 to 6.5.

Incorporate peat moss, leaf mold, or other well-rotted organic materials into the planting bed. Because European Evergreen Ginger is slow in becoming established as well as slow spreading, a mulch is necessary to help control weeds until cover is complete. A well-rotted, organic mulch of leaf mold or compost not only aids in weed control and moisture retention but also adds humus to the soil as it decomposes. Watering during dry periods assures a healthy planting.

In cold areas where there is not a continuous snow cover, European Evergreen Ginger should be planted so that it is protected from harsh winter winds and sun. Without protection, its evergreen leaves are subject to winter kill.

Plant in early spring. Space plants 8 to 12 inches apart.

Propagation is by division of the rhizomes in early spring before new growth starts.

Uses. European Evergreen Ginger is an excellent ground cover for use in shady areas because the glossy leaves reflect light. This plant can be used in masses beneath trees and shrubs, or combined with other shade-loving ground covers and wildflowers in a mixed planting.

Asaum europaeum is native to Europe.

Another excellent ginger ground cover is *Asarum shuttleworthii* (Mottled Wild Ginger). Its thick-textured, semievergreen to evergreen leaves are usually mottled with silver-gray, and are about 3 inches wide. The attractive flowers are urn-shaped, with broad, spreading lobes; the inside of the calyx is mottled violet. Growth rate is slow. *Asarum shuttleworthii* is native from the mountains of Virginia south to Alabama and Georgia and west to Tennessee, but is hardy beyond this range.

Brunnera macrophylla

Hardy Forget-me-not

Zone 3

Boraginaceae (Forget-me-not family)

Also known as Dwarf Anchusa, Heartleaf
Brunnera, Siberian Bugloss, Siberian
Forget-me-not

May be listed as *Anchusa myosotidiflora*,
Myosotis macrophylla

For a color illustration of *Brunnera macrophylla*,
see page 64.

Hardy Forget-me-not is a deciduous, somewhat rough, hairy, clump-forming perennial,
with stems arising from a central crown. The
leaves form a dense mound to 1 foot high. Growth
rate is slow. Texture is coarse.

Leaves. The almost blackish green leaves are
arranged alternately along the slender stems.
The basal leaves are large, long-petioled, egg-
shaped, and attached at the wide end to the
petiole. The leaf apex is sharply pointed, and
the base is shallowly lobed (cordate). Leaf size
and petiole length diminish with the height of
the stem until the upper leaves are about ½
the size of the basal leaves, and are very short-
petioled or lack a petiole (sessile). After the
plant flowers, the leaves increase in size until
they are 8 inches wide by midsummer, giving
the plant a somewhat coarse appearance.

Flowers. The small (⅛- to ¼-inch wide),
symmetrical, true-blue flowers resemble those
of *Myosotis* (True Forget-me-not). They are
borne in coiled, 1-sided cymes above the foliage.
The cymes uncoil as the flowers open. The
flowers are effective from April through June.
The overall effect is light and airy.

Culture. Hardy Forget-me-not will grow almost
anywhere, but grows best in full or partial shade
and in a moist, well-drained soil supplemented
with peat moss or well-rotted organic matter.
If the plant is grown in full sun, the leaves will
show signs of scorching by midsummer. In
poorly drained soils, crown rot may become
a problem.

Hardy Forget-me-not benefits from the
application of a well-rotted organic mulch in
the spring. Clumps that have deteriorated in the
center should be divided and reset early the
following spring. This plant is easily cultivated
and needs little care, expecially when properly
sited. Crowns should be set out in the spring.
Space 1½ to 2 feet apart.

Propagation is by seeds sown in the early
fall or by clump division in early spring. Plants
grown from seed will flower the following spring.
When grown in a suitable site, Hardy Forget-
me-not will often self-sow. These seedlings,
which may need to be removed to prevent
overcrowding, are a source of new plants.

Hardy Forget-me-not is commercially propagated by root cuttings of 1½-inch sections that
can be planted in the greenhouse in winter
or outside in early spring.

Uses. Hardy Forget-me-not is best used as a
ground cover in moist, shaded sites, woodland,
and naturalized areas. It combines well with
flowering bulbs and other spring ephemerals, its
foliage filling in to mask their disappearance.
This plant is valued for its true-blue flowers and
its hardiness.

Brunnera macrophylla is native to Siberia and
the Caucasus Mountains.

Campanula poscharskyana

Serbian Bellflower

Zone 3

Campanulaceae (Bellflower family)

Also known as Poscharsky Bellflower

Serbian Bellflower is a deciduous ground cover with a loose, creeping habit. It spreads rapidly, forming low masses of trailing stems that grow 6 to 9 inches high and may spread to 3 feet in diameter. The foliage is almost hidden in the spring by abundant, starlike flowers. Texture is medium-fine.

Leaves. The medium-green leaves are heart-shaped, sharp pointed at the apex, and coarsely toothed. They may be somewhat downy or glabrous (without hairs), and are 1 to 1½ inches long.

Flowers. The genus is characterized by bell-shaped, 5-lobed flowers (*Campanula* is Latin for "little bell"). The lavender-blue, starlike flowers of Serbian Bellflower are 1½ inches wide, and have deeply cut, pointed lobes that lie almost flat. They are produced abundantly from May through early June, and then sparsely throughout the remainder of the summer.

Culture. Serbian Bellflower will grow almost anywhere, and requires little care. It grows best in medium shade to full sun, and tolerates nearly any soil of moderate fertility as long as it is well drained. Do not plant in extremely hot, dry locations. A moist soil is desirable until the plant is well established; once established, Serbian Bellflower is drouth-tolerant, and is able to withstand neglect and relatively poor soils. An extremely fertile soil may cause growth that is too rampant and invasive.

For best results, apply a complete fertilizer annually in early spring and water during periods of drouth. Dig up and divide plantings that seem to have declined in vigor, and replant the strongest divisions.

Propagation is by seeds sown in the spring and by division. Divide the plants in early spring or late summer, and space these divisions 1 foot apart.

This plant is not usually seriously affected by insect pests or diseases, although leaf spots and powdery mildew may be troublesome.

Uses. Serbian Bellflower is often used as a trailing and clinging plant over dry walls. As a ground cover, it can be used effectively as a "filler" under shrubs, deciduous shade trees, and smaller, ornamental flowering trees. It should be planted where its flowers may be viewed at close range but in areas with little foot traffic. This plant is most valued for its rapid growth and attractive flowers.

Campanula poscharskyana is native to Dalmatia, a region of western Yugoslavia on the Adriatic Sea.

A closely related species that resembles a smaller, more refined Serbian Bellflower is *Campanula elatines* var. *garganica* (Adriatic or Dalmatian Bellflower). It is often listed and sold commercially as *Campanula garganica*. Smaller in every respect than Serbian Bellflower, this plant has grayish, hairy but shiny leaves, and its starry flowers are violet-blue with a white eye. Its cultural requirements and uses are the same as those of Serbian Bellflower. Space plants 6 to 8 inches apart.

Cerastium tomentosum

Snow-in-Summer

Zone 2

Caryophyllaceae (Pink family)

For a color illustration of *Cerastium tomentosum*, see page 65.

Snow-in-Summer is a vigorous, evergreen ground cover that forms soft mats of silvery foliage on erect stems up to 6 inches high. The flowers are borne above the foliage, and may reach 10 inches in height. The plant spreads rapidly by rhizomes. Texture is fine.

Leaves. The stems and simple, opposite leaves are densely covered with white hairs, giving the entire plant a frosted appearance. The leaves are ¾ to 1 inch long and about ¼ inch wide, with margins that are parallel or slightly broadened toward the base and taper to the apex.

Flowers. The complete, starry white flowers are ½ to ¾ inch wide, with 5 deeply notched petals. They are produced abundantly in May and June in 3 to 15 flowered cymes.

Culture. Snow-in-Summer is an adaptable, easily cultured plant. It needs full sun, and will thrive in any well-drained soil. A soil with moderate to low fertility is preferable because this plant grows vigorously and may become rampant in a highly fertile soil.

Snow-in-Summer should be watered until it is established. Once established, it is quite tolerant of periods of drouth; its appearance will be enhanced, however, if it is watered occasionally during these periods.

Snow-in-Summer spreads quickly to give complete coverage in a single growing season. One plant can easily cover an area of 2 to 3 square feet; in fertile soils, a single plant may even spread to 9 square feet. Its growth is so dense that weeds are not a problem. Applying fertilizer to the planting bed in areas with infertile soil will ensure good coverage.

If Snow-in-Summer is not maintained, it can become invasive and weedy. After flowering, or whenever plants become shabby or uneven in appearance, they should be cut back to rejuvenate growth and encourage compactness. As the flowers fade, the entire planting should be clipped or mowed with a rotary mower set at a height of 6 inches. Snow-in-Summer sows seed freely in unwanted areas if seed production is not eliminated. To rejuvenate deteriorating plants, cut the planting back almost to the ground, fertilize with a complete fertilizer, and water until vigorous growth is restored.

Plant in the spring. Space plants 10 to 12 inches apart.

Snow-in-Summer can be easily grown from seeds or cuttings taken after flowering. It can also be increased by division in early spring, when the plants are still dormant, or in early fall after they have ceased growth.

This plant is not seriously affected by insect pests or diseases.

Uses. Snow-in-Summer should be used either in areas where it has ample space to spread or where it can easily be restrained. It is an excellent ground cover for quickly covering rocky areas and banks in full sun. This plant can also be used as a "scrambler" over rock walls, as an edging plant, and as a filler between paving stones. It is valued for its silver-gray, evergreen foliage.

Cerastium tomentosum is native to southern Europe.

Ceratostigma plumbaginoides

Leadwort

Zone 5

Plumbaginaceae (Sea Lavender or Leadwort family)

Also known as Blue Leadwort, Chinese Leadwort, and Plumbago

May be listed as *Plumbago larpentae*

For a color illustration of *Ceratostigma plumbaginoides,* see page 65.

Leadwort is a deciduous to semievergreen ground cover that grows 8 to 12 inches high and forms masses of glossy green foliage on trailing, wiry stems 12 to 18 inches long. It spreads by slender rhizomes. Growth rate is moderate to fast. Texture is medium.

Leaves. The leaves are borne alternately on reddish, branching stems that often become woody at the base. They are egg-shaped, with the broader end toward the apex and the base tapering to the stem, and nearly sessile (stalkless). The leaves are about 3 inches long, and are glabrous (without hairs) except for the margin, which is ciliate (fringed with small, bristly hairs). The bright green foliage turns reddish bronze with the first frost in the autumn.

Flowers. The attractive, deep-blue flowers have a long season of bloom, flowering from early August until the first frost in the fall. The phloxlike corolla is a long, slender tube with 5 spreading lobes. The flowers are borne in dense terminal and axillary clusters. Each flower is ½ to ¾ inch wide, and is subtended by dry, papery, hairy-margined bracts. The sepals and bracts are persistent; their coppery or reddish color adds to the autumn effect of this plant.

Culture. Leadwort grows in sun or light shade in nearly any well-drained soil. If the soil is not rich in organic matter, incorporate peat moss, rotted compost, or other decayed materials into the planting bed.

In most of Zones 5 and 6, Leadwort dies to the ground in the winter, and will benefit from the application of a light mulch. This plant will not tolerate soggy soils; wet conditions in cold winter climates are fatal to it.

Leadwort resumes growth in mid-spring. The previous season's growth should be sheared almost to the ground in early spring to stimulate regrowth. Fertilize at this time with a low-nitrogen fertilizer such as 5-10-10. Once the new growth emerges, it is vigorous and fills in quickly.

Plant Leadwort only in the spring. Space plants 1½ to 2 feet apart.

Propagation is by division of clumps in the spring when new shoots first appear.

This plant is not seriously affected by insect pests or diseases.

Uses. Leadwort can be used as an underplanting for shrubs and small trees, in rock gardens, and as an edging plant. It is particularly valued for its blue flowers at a time of year when little else is flowering and for its attractive fall color.

Ceratogma plumbaginoides is native to western China.

Convallaria majalis

Lily-of-the-Valley

Zone 2

Liliaceae (Lily family)

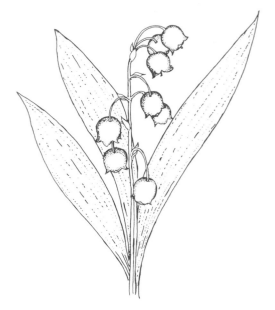

Lily-of-the-Valley is a deciduous ground cover that forms a thick carpet of upright and slightly arching leaves up to 8 inches high. It spreads rapidly by horizontal, underground rhizomes, creating a dense mass of soil-holding roots. In the spring, a single flower stalk arises from between the paired or tripled leaves to about the same height as the leaves but is not concealed by them. Texture is coarse.

Leaves. The dark-green leaves arise in pairs or occasionally triplets from "pips" (a section of the rhizome containing a bud). They are about 8 inches long, parallel-veined, and narrow to broadly elliptic. The foliage begins to deteriorate in late summer, and becomes progressively more unsightly until it dies down completely in the fall.

Flowers. The fragrant, waxy white flowers are borne in nodding, 1-sided racemes from mid-May to mid-June. They are pendant, about ¼ inch wide, and bell-shaped, with small, scalloped, slightly recurved lobes. At the base of each flower pedicel (stalk) is a small, narrow, leaflike bract. Lily-of-the-Valley is a favorite flower for wedding bouquets.

Fruits. Cross-pollination is necessary for fruiting. Most plantings of Lily-of-the-Valley arise from pips divided from a single plant, and fruits are seldom produced. The fruits are orange-red, pea-sized berries borne in the fall. They are poisonous, and should be removed if children are in the area.

Culture. This hardy, vigorous ground cover will grow almost anywhere, but grows best in a humus-rich, moist, well-drained soil in partial to full shade. When Lily-of-the-Valley is grown in full sun, the foliage browns and becomes "shabby" by midsummer; in hot, dry locations, the plant is subject to attack by spider mites.

Peat moss, leaf mold, or rotted compost should be incorporated into the planting bed and used as a mulch. To maintain attractive foliage, water the planting deeply during dry periods. Remove the previous season's foliage in early spring before new growth starts. Applying a complete fertilizer or 1 to 2 inches of organic matter each spring will improve the size and quality of the leaves and flowers, although the planting may be left undisturbed for many years as long as it appears healthy.

Overcrowding, which may occur after 4 to 5 years, causes a reduction in the number and quality of flowers. If flowering is an important ornamental feature of your planting, dig up and divide the pips, fertilize or incorporate organic matter into the bed, mulch, and replant the strongest divisions.

Plant in the spring. Space single pips 3 to 4 inches apart, and space larger divisions containing 2 or 3 pips 6 to 8 inches apart. A properly prepared and maintained bed should be entirely filled in after the second growing season.

Propagation is by division of the rhizomes in the spring.

Although generally free from insect pests and diseases, Lily-of-the-Valley may be attacked by spider mites, slugs, stem rot, or leaf spot.

Uses. Lily-of-the-Valley is an excellent ground cover for shady areas where little else will grow, and on shady banks and slopes, where its dense

roots aid in erosion control. If fertilized annually,
Lily-of-the-Valley competes well with tree roots,
and can be used effectively beneath shade trees
and shrubs. This plant combines well with
low-growing shrubs and ferns for a mixed
ground cover planting, although its late-season
foliage is unattractive. Do not use in areas
where it will crowd out more delicate plants.

Convallaria majalis is native to temperate
Europe, and is either native to or has become
naturalized in the mountainous regions of the
eastern United States. For centuries the roots and
rhizomes of Lily-of-the-Valley were used in
small doses to treat heart ailments. In larger
quantities, these parts are poisonous.

Recommended selections are ''Fortin's Giant',
'Fortunei', 'Prolificans', 'Florepleno', and 'Rosea'.
'Fortin's Giant' and 'Fortunei' have larger leaves
and flowers than the species; 'Prolificans' and
'Florepleno' have double flowers; and 'Rosea'
has pale pink flowers that fade badly if grown in
full sun. A variegated-foliage form, 'Aureo-
Variegata', has leaves that are striped longitudinally with creamy yellow. This cultivar is
rarely available commercially.

Coronilla varia

Crownvetch

Zone 3

Fabaceae of Leguminosae (Pea family)

For color illustrations of *Coronilla varia*, see page 65.

Crownvetch is commonly used on highway slopes throughout the Midwest. It is a sprawling, deciduous plant that mounds upon itself, forming masses 1 to 2 feet high. Spreading by underground stems, a single plant may cover an area 6 feet in diameter. Crownvetch is slow in becoming established; once established, however, it spreads rapidly and is difficult to eradicate. Texture is fine.

Leaves. The alternate, bright emerald-green leaves are pinnately compound (divided into 11 to 25 leaflets). The oblong, entire leaflets are ½ inch long. The foliage persists until December, reappearing about mid-spring.

Flowers. Crownvetch flowers from June to September. During much of this time, the foliage is blanketed with the pink and white, pealike blooms. They are produced in dense umbels on long peduncles that arise from the leaf axils. The complete flowers are about ½ inch long, with a 5-toothed calyx. The species name, *Coronilla,* the Latin word for "little crown," accurately describes the appearance of these flower clusters.

Culture. Crownvetch performs best in full sun but will tolerate light shade. This plant grows in almost any well-drained soil. In fertile soils, however, it grows rampantly and is difficult to control or eradicate (its optimum soil pH range is 6.0 to 7.5, and it will not tolerate a pH below 5.5). Crownvetch thrives in poor, dry sites, and is quite drouth-resistant after it is established.

Coverage is usually complete by the end of the second or third growing season. For roadside plantings, Crownvetch is commonly grown with a mulch or with a companion crop that germinates readily to aid in initial soil stabilization. Watering and a low-nitrogen fertilizer (such as 5-10-10) incorporated into the planting bed helps to accelerate establishment. Once established, Crownvetch provides a vigorous cover that requires little or no care.

After Crownvetch has become established, mow 2 to 3 times during the growing season for a neater, more compact planting. Set mower blades at least 6 inches high. Mow the planting to the ground in early winter to prevent the masses of dried stems and foliage from becoming a fire hazard and providing coverage for rodents.

Crownvetch is easily propagated by seeds and by division of the crowns. The seeds (like those of other legumes) should be inoculated with nitrogen-fixing bacteria. Sow seeds or plant seedlings in the spring at the rate of ½ pound per 1,000 square feet. Plant crowns or divisions in the spring or early fall. Crownvetch may self-seed into surrounding areas.

This rugged, durable plant is not seriously affected by insects or diseases.

Uses. Crownvetch is often used for soil stabilization on cuts and fills in poor, infertile soils where little else will grow. It controls sheet erosion on level ground, but is not effective in controlling gully erosion on steep slopes. This plant should be used in large areas with full sun; it is not suitable for the small landscape or for good soils in which other plants can be grown.

Coronilla varia is native to Europe, and has become naturalized over much of the northeastern United States.

Duchesnea indica

Mock Strawberry

Zone 3

Rosaceae (Rose family)

Also known as False Strawberry, Indian Strawberry

May be listed as *Fragaria indica*

Mock Strawberry is a semievergreen, trailing ground cover that grows to 6 inches high and can easily become rampant. This strawberrylike plant spreads by seeds (often carried by birds), and by sending out plantlet-producing runners that root at the nodes. Texture is medium.

Unfortunately, Mock Strawberry is often confused commercially with Barren Strawberry (*Waldsteinia ternata*, page 155), a highly desirable ground cover. Barren Strawberry may be distinguished from Mock Strawberry by its leaflets, flowers, and fruits. The leaflets of Barren Strawberry are wedge-shaped and rounded at the apex. The flowers are borne in 3- to 8-flowered corymbs, and each flower is subtended by 5 small, usually deciduous bracts. The fruits are inconspicuous brown achenes of no ornamental value.

Leaves. The bright green, long-petioled leaves are divided into 3 short-stalked leaflets. The leaflets are rhombic to egg-shaped, with a somewhat pointed apex and a margin that is coarsely serrate with blunt teeth. The leaves, petioles, and undersides of the leaflets are usually covered with silky hairs.

Flowers. The bright yellow flowers are produced from late April through most of the summer on long peduncles that arise singly from the leaf axils. The flowers are ½ to 1 inch in diameter, and are composed of 5 leafy sepals, 5 showy petals, and numerous stamens and pistils. Each flower is subtended by large, leafy, 3-lobed bracts that are alternate with the sepals. The bracts and calyx are persistent.

Fruits. The tasteless, strawberrylike "fruits" are produced from late June to early September.

They are about ½ inch wide, bright, glossy red, and highly ornamental. The surface of the swollen, red receptacle (commonly referred to as "the fruit") is studded with tiny, seedlike achenes (the true fruit).

Culture. Mock Strawberry is an Asiatic species that tolerates a wide range of growing conditions, and has become naturalized throughout most of eastern North America. It thrives in areas of full sun to almost full shade, and in almost any acid to neutral, well-drained soil. It establishes itself readily, with little bed preparation or care. Once established, Mock Strawberry tolerates drouth, heat, and neglect.

Because it is shallow rooted, Mock Strawberry may heave out of the ground in open winters, causing it to die out in spots. It regrows rapidly, however, and quickly fills in again to give complete coverage.

Propagation is by seeds or by separating rooted plantlets. Plant Mock Strawberry in the spring or early fall. Space plants 1 to 1½ feet apart.

Uses. Mock Strawberry should be used only in areas where its rampant growth can be completely restricted (in island planters, beside concrete walks, etc.).

Duchesnea indica is native to Southern Asia, and has become naturalized in North America from New York to Iowa and southward. Some states list Mock Strawberry as a noxious weed. Ironically, this plant was named to commemorate Antoine Nicolas Duchesne, an eighteenth-century horticulturist who was one of the foremost authorities on true strawberries.

Epimedium species

Epimedium

Berberidaceae (Barberry family)

Also known as Barrenwort, Bishop's Hat

For a color illustration of *Epimedium* species, see page 65.

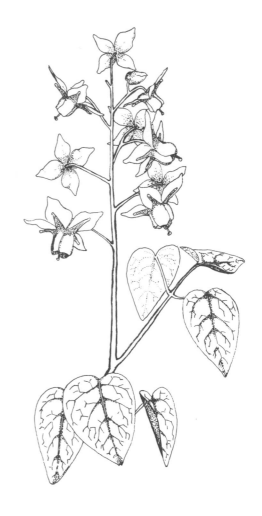

The genus *Epimedium* consists of about 25 species and hybrids of low-growing, clump-forming, and spreading perennials. Epimediums spread by somewhat woody rhizomes. The clump-forming epimediums are often more delicate in habit than the spreading types, and are more appropriately used as accent or specimen plants. The species that are most suitable for ground covers spread vigorously by elongated rhizomes to form an extremely uniform cover. The rate of spread is moderate.

Leaves. The foliage of epimediums is generally deciduous to semievergreen. The leaves of those species considered semievergreen are persistent into the winter months, but are usually badly browned and tattered by spring. A few species are truly evergreen.

The leaves of all species are compound, and are borne on stiff, wiry petioles. In some species, the leaves are divided into 3 leaflets (ternate); in others, each leaflet is again divided into 3 leaflets (biternate). The leaves may all be basal (arising directly from the rhizomes), or they may be mostly basal with an additional single leaf on the flowering stalks. Some hybrids have both leafless and leafy flowering stalks.

Although leathery in texture, the leaflets appear delicate. They are heart-shaped or somewhat triangular, tapering to a fine point at the apex, and are usually margined with slender, spine-tipped teeth. (In a few species, the leaflets are smooth edged.) The newly emerged leaflets of some species and hybrids have rosy red veins and margins; the leaflets turn a uniform green by summer. Some species and hybrids take on attractive red or bronze coloration in the fall.

Flowers. The flowers of epimediums are complete, and are borne in loose, terminal racemes on slender stalks as the new foliage develops in May or June. The dainty, drooping or nodding flowers are of an unusual construction. All flower parts are in series of 4. The first whorl of flower parts, at the point of attachment to the pedicel (flower stalk), consists of 4 outer sepals that are small and inconspicuous and usually drop off as the flower opens. The second whorl consists of 4 colorful inner sepals that function as petals and vary greatly from species to species. The third whorl consists of 4 petals. In most species, these are spurred or hooded, and function as nectaries (glands that secrete nectar). The spurs may be short, enclosed by the inner sepals, or long and showy, extending out beyond the inner sepals. The bases of the petals are often flattened, forming a cuplike structure around the stamens. The flowers are long lasting when cut, and are attractive additions to bouquets and arrangements.

Fruits. Epimediums are probably self-sterile. Because most plantings consist of plants from a single clone, fruit is seldom set.

Culture. These plants grow best in partial to fairly deep shade in a moist, well-drained soil that is rich in humus. They will also grow in sunny locations if the soil is kept moist, but will not tolerate dry soils.

Incorporate well-rotted organic matter (compost, leaf mold, or decayed manure) into the planting bed to a depth of at least 12 inches; apply again as a mulch about 2 inches deep each spring. If epimediums are grown where they compete with trees and shrubs for soil nutrients, they should also receive an annual spring application of a complete fertilizer.

Cut away the foliage remaining from the previous season's growth in late winter or very early spring before new growth starts. Water during dry periods. Do not cultivate around these plants; they are shallow rooted, and may be damaged easily. Epimediums require little care, and their attractive, durable foliage is essentially pest free.

Epimediums are most easily propagated by division after the foliage has matured. Divide the plants in the spring or early summer; space the divisions (or purchased plants) 9 to 12 inches apart. Except for propagation purposes, epimediums can be left undisturbed indefinitely.

Uses. Epimediums are among the best herbaceous ground-cover plants. They can be used effectively in small groupings, as rock-garden specimens, and under trees where grass will not grow.

Epimedium species are native primarily to China and Japan. A few species are found in Europe, Asia Minor, and northern Africa. The common name "Barrenwort" refers to the root extract of a plant confused with Epimedium that was believed to prevent conception in women. The common name "Bishop's Hat" resulted from the resemblance of the 4-pointed, squarish flowers to a clergyman's biretta.

The *Epimedium* species and hybrids described on pages 96-98 are suitable for use as ground covers in the Midwest. Unfortunately, the botanical nomenclature of epimediums is confused, and these plants are often listed in catalogs under obsolete or incorrect names. They can be correctly identified, however, from accurate flower descriptions or by actually seeing the plants in flower.

Epimedium alpinum

Alpine Epimedium

Zone 3

Epimedium grandiflorum

Long-spur Epimedium

Zone 3

May be listed as *Epimedium macranthum*

Alpine Epimedium grows 1 to 1½ feet high. The biternate leaves are basal, arising from the rhizomes. The leaflets are up to 5 inches long, giving this plant a somewhat coarse appearance. New spring growth is red tinged. The foliage persists late in the year but emerges from the winter severely battered or dead.

The flowers are not as showy as those of many of the other epimediums. The inflorescence is partially hidden by the foliage, and the flowers are quite small (up to ½ inch in diameter). The inner sepals are a dull or rose red, and are longer than the short, spurred yellow petals that they partially enclose. The bases of the petals do not form a cup, and the stamens protrude conspicuously.

Alpine Epimedium is seldom offered commercially. Most of the plants sold under this name are actually *Epimedium × rubrum,* a hybrid resulting from a cross between *Epimedium alpinum* and *Epimedium grandiflorum* that most closely resembles *Epimedium alpinum* (see page 97).

Long-spur Epimedium, although exceptionally attractive, has contributed to a number of hybrids that have overshadowed it in popularity. The delicate foliage (the leaflets are spine-margined and about 1 inch wide) grows 1 foot high. The leaves are basal, with leafy flowering stalks. The new spring foliage is tinted reddish; autumn coloration is bronze. Although deciduous, the foliage persists late into the season.

The flowers are among the largest (1 to 2 inches in diameter) and showiest of the epimediums. The inflorescence of spiderlike blooms is borne just above the foliage. The outer sepals are red, and the inner sepals are violet. The conspicuous petals are white and long spurred. The spurs curve backward, and are nearly twice as long as the inner sepals. The bases of the petals are tinged violet and are well developed, obscuring the stamens.

The cultivar *Epimedium grandiflorum* 'Violaceum' is more widely cultivated and generally available than the species. It is often listed as *Epimedium grandiflorum violaceum* and *Epimedium violaceum.* The flowers of this plant are a uniform light violet, and the spurs of the petals are only slightly longer than the inner sepals.

Epimedium pinnatum

Persian Epimedium

Zone 5

Epimedium × rubrum

Red Epimedium

Zone 4

Also known as Red Alpine Epimedium

May be listed as *Epimedium alpinum,
Epimedium alpinum rubrum*

For a color illustration of *Epimedium × rubrum*, see page 66.

Persian Epimedium is sometimes confused with *Epimedium × versicolor* (see page 98). Its all-basal foliage grows to about 1 foot high, and is persistent, although not evergreen. The leaves are biternate, and the leaflets are spine-margined.

The inflorescences rise above the foliage to about 1½ feet high, and are quite showy. The flowers are about ⅝ inch in diameter, with large, bright yellow inner sepals. The small, short-spurred petals are brownish red; their bases do not form a cuplike structure, and the stamens are prominently exposed.

Epimedium pinnatum var. *colchicum* is more often found in cultivation than the species. The leaves of this plant have fewer leaflets than those of the species (usually 3 or 5), and the leaflets are almost spineless. The spurs of the petals are also somewhat longer than those of the species. This plant may be listed as *Epimedium colchicum, Epimedium elegans,* and *Epimedium pinnatum elegans.*

Red Epimedium is the most widely cultivated epimedium. The foliage is persistent but not evergreen. It is edged and veined with red in the spring, becoming green but retaining its red margin when mature. Autumn coloration is bronzish.

The showy inflorescences rise above the foliage. The flowers are about 1 inch wide, with conspicuous, bright crimson inner sepals. The spurred petals are creamy white tinged with red; the spurs are upcurved slightly, and are as long as the inner sepals. The bases of the petals form a shallow cup that partially encloses the stamens.

Red Epimedium is a hybrid resulting from a cross between *Epimedium alpinum* and *Epimedium grandiflorum,* and most closely resembles *Epimedium alpinum* (see page 96).

Epimedium × versicolor

Zone 4

The foliage of *Epimedium × versicolor* is persistent but not evergreen, and forms a mass about 1 foot high. The spring growth is mottled red, and the autumn foliage is tinged pinkish red.

The flowers are about 1 inch wide, and are borne in nodding sprays above the foliage. The inner sepals are rose, and the spurred petals are yellow with red-tinged spurs. The bases of the petals are well developed, forming a cup enclosing the stamens.

Epimedium × versicolor is a hybrid resulting from a cross between *Epimedium grandiflorum* and *Epimedium pinnatum,* and most closely resembles *Epimedium pinnatum* (see page 97).

The cultivar *Epimedium × versicolor* 'Sulphureum' is more common in cultivation than the hybrid, and is one of the most readily available epimediums. It is distinguished by its pale yellow inner sepals and uniformly bright yellow, spurred petals. Its spring foliage is generally unmottled. This cultivar may also be listed as *Epimedium luteum, Epimedium ochroleucum, Epimedium pinnatum sulphureum,* and *Epimedium sulphureum.*

Festuca ovina var. *glauca*

Blue Fescue

Zone 4

Poaceae or Gramineae (Grass family)

May also be listed as *Festuca glauca*

For a color illustration of *Festuca ovina* var. *glauca*, see page 66.

Blue Fescue is a clump-forming, ornamental grass that grows 6 to 10 inches high in distinct, rounded tufts of evergreen, silvery blue foliage. The flowers grow on stems well above the foliage to almost 2 feet high. Growth rate is rapid. Texture is fine.

Leaves. The leaves are borne on densely clustered, silvery blue stems. They are narrow and grasslike, fine-pointed, and nearly rolled into slender tubes. The foliage color may vary from light blue to blue-green and silvery blue.

Flowers. The small, buff-colored flowers are produced in narrow, spikelike panicles from early June to early July. The panicles are less than 4 inches long, and overtop the foliage on slender stalks up to 20 inches long. The flowers are not ornamental.

Culture. Blue Fescue should be grown in full sun in a well-drained soil. It will grow in light to medium shade, but attains its bluest foliage color and most uniform growth in full sun.

This plant is tolerant of infertile, dry soils. When Blue Fescue is grown in wet, poorly drained, clay soils, however, the centers of the clumps die out quickly, and the plants must be dug, divided, and replanted every 1 or 2 years. When properly sited in a well-drained soil, the planting requires division and replanting only as the tufts deteriorate.

Mow or cut back the clumps in early spring before new growth begins. To stimulate new growth, cut back "shabby" clumps at any time during the growing season. Regrowth is rapid, and the clumps fill in quickly.

Because Blue Fescue does not form a solid cover, it must be used in combination with a mulch in order to control weeds. It is particularly attractive with rock mulches.

Propagation is by division of the clumps in spring or early fall. Plant at the same time that the clumps are divided. Space plants 9 to 12 inches apart, depending upon the effect that you want to achieve.

This plant is not seriously affected by insect pests or diseases.

Uses. Blue Fescue is widely used as a border or edging plant or as an accent plant in rock gardens. As a ground cover, Blue Fescue is used to form geometric or other stylized patterns, and is especially effective in full sun on rocky, gentle (it will not control erosion), well-drained slopes. This plant is valued for its silvery blue year-round foliage color.

Festuca ovina var. *glauca* is native to Eurasia, and has become naturalized in temperate North America.

Helictotrichon sempervirens (Blue Oat Grass) closely resembles Blue Fescue, and has similar uses in the landscape. This gracefully arching plant grows 2 to 3 feet high, and is about 4 feet high when in flower. Its light, silvery blue leaves are ½ to 1½ feet long, and are tightly rolled and fine-pointed. The purplish flowers are borne in loose panicles from 2 to 7 inches long. Blue Oat Grass is hardy to Zone 5, and is semi-evergreen in its more northern range or in open areas. It is sometimes listed as *Avena candida*.

Filipendula vulgaris

Dropwort

Zone 4

Rosaceae (Rose family)

Also known as Meadowsweet

May be listed as *Filipendula hexapetala, Spiraea filipendula*

For color illustrations of *Filipendula vulgaris* and *Filipendula vulgaris* 'Flore Pleno', see page 66.

Dropwort is a long-cultivated perennial that forms dense, basal tufts of fernlike, evergreen foliage that grow 1 to 1½ feet high and up to 1½ feet wide. The flowers are borne on erect, leafy stems 2 to 3 feet high that emerge from the centers of the foliage tufts. The rate of spread is moderate to rapid. Texture is fine.

Leaves. When the plant is not in flower, the basal foliage rosette may be mistaken for a fern. The slender leaves are ½ to 1½ feet long and 2 inches or less wide. Each leaf is divided into 8 to 25 pairs of narrowly oblong leaflets about 1 inch long. The leaflets are pinnately lobed, and the lobes are finely toothed. The flowering stem leaves are alternate and smaller than the basal leaves.

Flowers. The small, creamy white flowers are ¾ inch wide, and are crowded in branched, terminal, plumelike clusters that grow up to 4 inches wide. The undersides of the petals are pinkish purple, and the blooms appear pink when in bud. The flowers are borne from early to mid-July.

Culture. Dropwort is a durable plant that grows best in partial shade but will grow in full sun if the soil is somewhat moist. Almost any soil of moderate fertility is suitable. This plant will thrive in poor soils if moisture is adequate and if it is fertilized occasionally.

Although Dropwort tolerates dry soils better than the other members of this genus, moist spring soils will produce better flowering. In soggy soils, mildew may deteriorate the foliage.

Maintenance requirements are minimal. Dropwort benefits from a light application of a complete fertilizer in early spring. For additional plant vigor, remove the flower stalks as the flowers fade. Plantings are virtually permanent. They occasionally become overcrowded, resulting in inferior flowering, and it may be necessary to divide or mechanically thin the clumps and replant them.

Propagation is by seeds sown in the fall and by division of the clumps or tubers (enlarged, fleshy portions of the underground stems) in the spring. Space plants 2 feet apart.

Uses. This plant has traditionally been used in the flower border. When massed, Dropwort is a desirable, rugged ground cover for almost any partially shaded location.

Filipendula vulgaris is native to the dry grasslands of Europe and western Asia. An oil similar to oil of wintergreen has been distilled from the flowers, and the aromatic leaves have been used in cold remedies and to flavor soups.

A recommended selection is the double-flowering cultivar *Filipendula vulgaris* 'Flore Pleno'. This plant is 15 to 18 inches high when it is in flower. It is preferable to the species because of its more compact habit and showier, longer lasting flowers.

Galium odoratum

Sweet Woodruff

Zone 4

Rubiaceae (Madder family)

Also known as Sweet Woodroof, Woodruff

May be listed as *Asperula odorata*

For a color illustration of *Galium odoratum*, see page 66.

Sweet Woodruff is a delicate appearing, deciduous ground cover (evergreen in warmer climates) that forms mats of foliage of almost uniform height (6 to 8 inches high). Although this plant is deciduous, the bright green foliage persists late into the fall and reppears early the following spring. The flowers are borne 8 to 10 inches high, and grow above the foliage. The plant spreads rapidly by creeping underground stems. Texture is fine.

Leaves. The leaves are borne on square stems in whorls of 6 to 8 that are about 1 inch apart. The very finely serrate leaves are stalkless (sessile), 1 to 1½ inches long, elliptic, and bristle-tipped.

Flowers. The small white flowers are about ¼ inch wide, with a corolla that is deeply divided into 4 parts. They are borne in loose, branching, terminal cymes in May and June, and blanket the foliage for several weeks.

Culture. Sweet Woodruff should be planted in medium to deep shade. It will grow in almost any soil, but grows best in a moist, well-drained, humus-rich, somewhat acid soil. Incorporate peat moss or well-rotted organic matter into the planting bed. Supplemental watering is necessary until the planting is well established. After Sweet Woodruff is established, it needs to be watered only during dry periods.

For best flowering, fertilize in early spring with a low-nitrogen fertilizer such as 5-10-10. The planting may be sheared lightly several times during the growing season to obtain a formal effect.

Plant in the spring. Space plants 10 to 12 inches apart. When Sweet Woodruff is properly sited, the foliage remains in good condition throughout the growing season. Plantings are dense, long-lived, and rarely need thinning.

This plant is not seriously affected by insect pests or diseases.

Uses. Sweet Woodruff is an excellent plant for moist shade, expecially deep shade where little else will grow. It combines well with English Ivy for a mixed ground-cover bed, as well as with spring flowering bulbs. Although Sweet Woodruff requires occasional fertilization, it thrives under shallow-rooted shrubs and trees. This plant is valued for its uniform growth, attractive, persistent foliage, and relatively long blooming period.

Sweet Woodruff is most easily propagated by division in early spring, although satisfactory results may be obtained by division almost anytime during the growing season.

Galium odoratum is native to Europe and western Asia. The dried leaves and stems are strongly aromatic (reminiscent of newmown hay), and are used for sachets. It is also used to flavor May wine and other beverages.

Geranium species

Geranium

Geraniaceae (Geranium family)

Also known as Cranesbill

For a color illustration of *Geranium* species, see page 67.

Geraniums are deciduous, mound- to clump-forming plants with trailing or erect stems. They seldom grow more than 1½ feet high, and spread moderately to rapidly by rhizomes. All geraniums produce colorful, showy flowers that are held above the foliage mass. Most species also have attractive leaves that take on reddish and bronze colorations in the autumn. Several species are widely cultivated in Europe, where they are often used as ground covers. These plants are true geraniums, and should not be confused with the annual bedding plants with large flower clusters that are commonly offered commercially as geraniums, and that belong to the related genus *Pelargonium*. The texture of these plants ranges from fine to medium.

Leaves. The foliage and stems of geraniums are usually somewhat hairy. The round to kidney-shaped leaves are palmately lobed or divided (often deeply divided), and the lobes are generally coarsely toothed. The basal leaves are long-petioled; the upper leaves are usually short-petioled.

Flowers. Some species of geraniums flower from mid- to late spring; others continue to flower throughout most of the summer. The complete flowers are 1 to 2 inches wide, with 5 slightly overlapping, showy petals of varying shades of pink or purple. They may be solitary or paired, arising from the leaf axils or in terminal clusters.

Fruits. The fruits are long, slender capsules that open explosively when mature, dispersing seeds in all directions. The 5-parted calyx subtending the fruits is persistent. (The name "geranium" is derived from *geranos*, the Greek word for "crane," and refers to the long, beaklike fruits.)

Culture. Geraniums are easy to grow, and thrive in almost any well-drained soil of average fertility with a pH range of 6.0 to 8.0. They grow well in sun or light shade, flowering most profusely in full sun. Do not plant in wet or extremely fertile soils, and do not overfertilize. High fertility results in excessive spreading and leggy, unattractive growth. The plants will have a more compact habit and may flower better in a somewhat infertile soil.

In general, these plants need little care. They should be fertilized in early spring with a complete fertilizer. Although geraniums are somewhat drouth-tolerant, for best appearance they should be watered during extended dry periods. Some species may be cut back about ⅓ to ½ after flowering to encourage repeat flowering later in the season, and to produce more compact growth and a faster rate of spread. The blooming period for some other species can be extended by removing the flowers as they fade. Many species of geraniums self-sow invasively, and it may be beneficial to eliminate seed production by removing the faded flowers.

Geraniums need to be thinned or divided when they begin to deteriorate. Deterioration may occur every 4 to 5 years for some species; others are much longer lived or may never require thinning. The plants should be thinned in the spring; the divisions may also serve as a means of propagation.

Geranium species can be propagated by seeds that germinate in 1 to 5 weeks, but cultivars and hybrids should be propagated by division in the spring or by stem cuttings taken in the summer. Spring division is the easiest and most reliable method of propagation for all geraniums. Plant in the spring. Space plants 8 to 12 inches apart.

These plants are seldom seriously affected by insect pests or diseases. In cool, moist conditions, however, leaf spots and botrytis blight may be troublesome. The 4-lined plant bug may also be a problem. Ask your county Extension adviser for control recommendations.

Uses. Geraniums can be used effectively in the flower border and rock garden. They also combine well with wildflowers, and are excellent plants for naturalistic settings. When massed, they make an excellent, hardy ground cover adaptable to many locations. They are valued for their lovely flowers, long blooming period, and adaptability.

Geranium species are widely distributed. They are primarily found in temperate and mountainous regions of the world.

Geranium cinereum

Gray Cranesbill

Zone 4

Gray Cranesbill is a low, mounded plant that grows to about 6 inches high. The leaves, which are covered with a whitish wax, appear gray. They are 5- to 7-lobed; the lobes are cut nearly to the center and deeply toothed.

The flower peduncles are either axillary or arise from the root crown. The paired flowers are pink with dark veins and about 1 inch wide. Flower color varies from pale pink to lilac or purplish pink. Gray Cranesbill flowers in June and July.

Geranium cinereum 'Album' is a cultivar with white flowers. 'Splendens' is a dwarf, growing to about 3 inches high, and has deep pink flowers.

Geranium endressii

Endres Cranesbill

Zone 4

Endres Cranesbill is a densely hairy, clump-forming plant that grows to 1½ feet high and spreads rapidly. The long-petioled leaves are mostly basal, arising from the rhizomes. They are 2 to 3 inches wide and very deeply 5-lobed (cleft nearly to the leaf base).

The small, rose-colored flowers are produced abundantly in May. They are ½ inch wide, and are borne in pairs on axillary peduncles. Cut the flowers back after flowering for a repeat blooming in the summer.

Geranium himalayense

Lilac Cranesbill

Zone 3

May be listed as *Geranium grandiflorum*

Lilac Cranesbill forms 1-foot-wide clumps of stout, hairy, ascending stems that grow 1 to 1½ feet high. The long-petioled leaves are usually up to 3 inches wide but may be wider. They are deeply cut into 5 to 7 coarsely and irregularly toothed lobes.

The flowers are 1½ inches wide, and are held mostly above the foliage. The showy petals are lilac with darker purple veins; the peduncles are axillary, up to 8 inches long, and usually 2-flowered. Lilac Cranesbill blooms from May into July.

Geranium ibericum

Iberian Cranesbill

Zone 3

Also known as Caucasus Geranium

For a color illustration of *Geranium ibericum* 'Album', see page 67.

Iberian Cranesbill is a hairy, clump-forming geranium with thick rhizomes and stout stems that grow to 1½ feet high. The erect stems are leafless below and branching, with leaves arranged oppositely above. The leaves are 2 to 6 inches wide and 7-lobed (cleft nearly to the leaf base); the lobes are deeply and coarsely toothed. A few long-stalked leaves arise from the rhizomes, but most leaves are borne on the stems. The foliage turns reddish with the first hard frost.

The violet-blue, 2-inch-wide flowers overtop the foliage. They are produced during July and August in open, few-flowered, terminal panicles. The petals are 1¼ inches long, and are slightly notched at their apices.

Geranium ibericum 'Album' is a white-flowered cultivar.

Geranium sanguineum

Bloodred Geranium

Zone 3

Also known as Bloody Cranesbill

For a color illustration of *Geranium sanguineum*, see page 67.

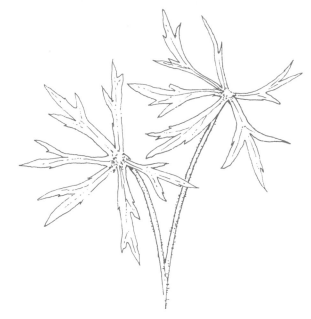

Bloodred Geranium is mounded in habit, with more or less trailing stems that spread to 2 feet or more in diameter. The mounds are about 1½ feet high when the plant is in flower. The leaves are 1½ to 2 inches wide, and are borne mostly along stems that are covered with white hairs. They are 5- to 7-lobed (cleft nearly to the leaf base); each lobe is divided into fingerlike lobules. Texture is medium-fine. The common names of this plant refer to its scarlet red foliage color that appears after the first hard frost.

The 1- to 1½-inch-wide flowers are axillary and solitary. They are usually bright magenta, although they may vary in color to shades of pink and purple. Bloodred Geranium flowers profusely for approximately 45 days from early June to August. It may self-sow. After flowering, cut the plants back about ⅓ to remove seed capsules and promote more rapid spread.

Geranium sanguineum var. *prostratum* (Dwarf Bloodred Geranium) grows only 6 inches high, forming a spreading mound 18 inches wide or wider. This variety may also be listed as *Geranium lancastrense*. The cultivar *Geranium sanguineum* 'Album' is a white-flowered form.

Hemerocallis species

Daylily

Liliaceae (Lily family)

Hemerocallis genus is composed of approximately 15 species of clump-forming, evergreen to deciduous perennials that form large masses (usually 1 to 2 feet high) of gracefully ascending to arching, grasslike foliage. Daylilies have large, fibrous root systems, often with fleshy, tuberous enlargements. They spread by rhizomes that may be very short, forming compact, slowly creeping clumps, or as long as 5 to 12 inches. The clustered flowers are commonly borne in the summer on leafless stalks that range in height from 1½ to 8 feet. Rate of spread is moderate to rapid. Texture is medium-fine to medium-coarse.

Leaves. The dark-green, linear leaves vary from 5 to 14 inches to 2 to 4 feet long, depending upon the species. They are basal (arising from the crown) and 2-ranked, forming fans of foliage. The leaves are entire, with a sharp- to blunt-pointed apex and a distinct midrib along which the leaf is folded, most prominently toward the base.

Flowers. Daylilies bloom from late spring into September. The complete, lilylike flowers are borne in terminal clusters on erect, bracted, slender stalks that arise from the center of the crown. There are few to numerous symmetrical flowers per stalk. Each flower has 6 perianth segments that are slightly united basally and arranged in 2 whorls of 3; the 3 outer segments are petallike sepals that alternate with the 3 inner petals. The perianth may vary from flaring and funnel-shaped to nearly bell-shaped; the segments are elliptical, oblong, or spoon-shaped, and are often recurved and ruffled. There are 6 stamens and a single pistil with a long, slender style. The flower colors range from various shades of yellow to orange, brownish orange, and red. Although individual flowers bloom for only a day (*Hemerocallis* is derived from the Greek words meaning "beautiful for a day"), the plants remain in flower for up to 4 weeks as a succession of buds mature and open. The flowers of some species are noted for their night blooming, opening in late afternoon and remaining open until the next day.

Fruits. The fruits are 3-chambered capsules that split open as they mature and dry.

Culture. Daylilies are quite easy to grow. They are adaptable to many areas, although they grow best in full sun to light shade in a well-drained soil to which organic matter has been added. The flowers of some species may fade, burn, or wilt in sunny, very hot areas. These species are best grown in light shade. All daylilies are tolerant of heavier shade but flowering will be reduced. Although they tolerate periods of very wet weather, continuously soggy soils are detrimental.

Daylilies are rugged, durable plants that will survive considerable neglect but respond admirably to favorable conditions. Incorporate 2 to 4 inches of organic matter in the form of leaf mold, well-rotted compost or manure into the planting bed. One to 2 inches of organic matter applied annually as a mulch will furnish the planting with its nutrient requirements as the mulch decomposes, usually making fertilization unnecessary.

Plants growing in very poor or sandy soils where nutrients are readily leached may need to be fertilized lightly with a complete fertilizer 2 to 3 times during the spring and summer. Daylilies should be fertilized sparingly, and only after they are well established. Overfertilization can cause excessive vegetative growth and poor flowering.

Because of their large, often fleshy root systems, daylilies can survive prolonged periods of drouth. Inadequate moisture when the flower stalks and buds are forming will result in inferior flowering, however, and the planting should be watered thoroughly. Soak the planting to a depth of about 10 inches. Allow the soil to dry out before watering again.

To maintain best appearance, cut and remove the flower stalks after all the flowers have faded. Some evergreen types may be grown in cold winter climates, but they require winter protection and a loose winter mulch (see page 7). Evergreen daylilies grow best south of Zone 6. The foliage of the more reliable deciduous daylilies dies to the ground in the autumn. It may be left on the planting to serve as a winter mulch, and then raked off in early spring before new growth begins. Very vigorously spreading daylilies may be contained by growing them in confined areas, or by cutting around the planting with a sharp spade and removing any rhizomes that have spread out of bounds. Some plantings may eventually become overcrowded and require thinning to restore vigor and increase flower production.

Propagation is usually by division of clumps. Although the clumps may be divided at any time during the growing season, it is best to divide them in early spring or after flowering in late August through mid-September. Those species that flower very late should be divided in the spring. Each division should contain 1 to several healthy fans of foliage (ramets); a single ramet division will not flower well during the first or perhaps even second year. The leaves should be cut back to 8 to 10 inches. Remove any broken or damaged roots.

Some daylilies may produce proliferations (leafy shoots) on their flowering stalks. These proliferations can be air-layered or removed and rooted in sand. If you keep them well watered,

they should be rooted in a few weeks. Although daylilies may also be propagated by seeds, seedlings require 2 to 3 years to flower and are subject to wide variation. Commercial growers use several other methods of vegetative propagation (such as tissue culture and vertical crown sections) to increase their stock quickly.

It is preferable to plant daylilies in the spring, late summer, and early fall, although they may be planted whenever the soil is workable. Space plants up to 3 feet apart, depending upon the species, size of the plants, and rate of spread. Plant so that the crown of the plant (where the leaves meet the roots) is 1 inch below the soil surface. Planting too deeply may cause a loss of vigor, poor flowering, and discoloration of the foliage.

Daylilies are seldom seriously affected by insect pests and diseases. Thrips are probably the most troublesome pest, and slugs, aphids, spider mites, Japanese beetles, root-knot nematodes, blight (withering of the flowering stalks), and russet spot on leaves have all been reported. If necessary, ask your county Extension adviser for appropriate control measures.

Uses. The landscape potential of daylilies has been largely overlooked. Because of their tolerance, persistence, and easy maintenance, these plants can be used in many locations, and they are attractive even when they are not in flower. Some species have extensive root systems and vigorous spreading qualities that make them suitable for erosion control and for use in large, informal areas and naturalistic settings. Daylilies can also be used effectively on slopes or stream banks, around ponds, and along driveways, railroad tracks, and highways. They may also be used as foundation plantings and in the perennial border.

Hemerocallis species are native from Europe to China and Japan. The species have largely been supplanted commercially by thousands of superior hybrids. The American Hemerocallis Society (ask your county Extension adviser for the address) offers many publications dealing with daylilies.

Daylilies are important in the Chinese diet. The flowers are dried for use in soups and stews, and the larger flower buds and newly opened flowers are dipped in batter and deep fried. The tuberous root enlargements of certain species have a nutlike taste, and can be eaten raw, fried, or boiled in salt water. Certain medicinal properties have also been attributed to daylilies.

Hemerocallis fulva

Tawny Daylily

Zone 2

Also known as Brown Daylily, Corn Daylily, Fulvous Daylily, Homestead Lily, Orange Daylily

For color illustrations of *Hemerocallis fulva*, see page 67.

Tawny Daylily is a persistent, long-lived daylily that is native to Eruope and Asia. It was brought to this country by the earliest settlers, and has become naturalized throughout the eastern United States.

This robust plant spreads rapidly by elongated rhizomes to form broad masses of dense foliage. It is sometimes considered a weed because it can choke out more delicate plants and is difficult to eradicate. Texture is somewhat coarse.

The fans of foliage are composed of ascending and arching leaves that are 1½ to 2 feet long and about 1⅜ inches wide. The flower stalks may grow to 6 feet high but are usually 4 to 5 feet high, and bear 6 to 12 flowers per stalk. The odorless, brownish to rusty orange-red flowers are 3½ inches wide and almost 5 inches long. Tawny Daylily flowers in July.

Many authorities believe that most of the Tawny Daylilies grown in the United States are *Hemerocallis fulva* 'Europa'. This cultivar is a sterile triploid that does not produce fruits; however, it produces viable pollen that has been used extensively in hybridization to impart vigor and produce red flower colorations.

Another common form of Tawny Daylily is the double-flowering cultivar 'Kwanso'. It is slightly coarser than Tawny Daylily, with leaves up to 2 inches wide that may be occasionally striped with white. This plant flowers just after Tawny Daylily, and is also sterile. *Hemerocallis fulva* 'Kwanso' may also be listed as *Hemerocallis fulva* 'Flore Pleno', *Hemerocallis fulva* var. *kwanso,* and *Hemerocallis kwanso.*

Two other cultivars that have been used widely in hybridization are 'Cypriana' and 'Rosea'. 'Cypriana' has many coppery red flowers per stalk. Each flower has a golden eye, and is marked with gold along the midvein of the inner segments. 'Rosea' has rosy red flowers and dark-green leaves that are narrower than those of the species.

Hemerocallis hybrids

Hybrid Daylilies

Zone 3

For a color illustration of a *Hemerocallis* hybrid, see page 68.

Few hybrid daylilies were known before the twentieth century. Thanks largely to the efforts of American hybridizers, however, there are now thousands of hybrid daylilies available that are far superior to the species. Often termed varieties, these hybrids are more correctly labeled cultivars (see page 11), and are usually the result of crosses of hybrids. Commercially worthy cultivars are named (for example, *Hemerocallis* 'Hyperion'), registered, and introduced into the market. The prices of these new cultivars are usually quite high the first year, but decrease rapidly as stocks increase. New propagation methods, such as tissue culture, are helping increase stocks very quickly, and should help to hold introductory prices down in the future. The newest introductions are perhaps best left to the specialists and collectors until they have proved their merit.

Most commercially available hybrids range from 1½ to 5 feet high at the time of flowering, and are promoted largely on the basis of floral characteristics. When selecting cultivars for use as ground covers, however, you should also consider foliage color and vigor. The foliage colors include various shades of green, grayish green, and bluish green. Choose cultivars that are not prone to yellowing and leaf spots. Long rhizomes, with their accompanying invasiveness, have mostly been bred out of daylily cultivars, and these plants are now generally permanent and noninvasive.

The diversity in floral characteristics of daylilies is nearly overwhelming, encompassing greatly expanded color choices and patterns, flower forms and sizes, and blooming time. The flowers range in size from 3 to 8 inches wide, and in color from near-white to virtually every shade of yellow, orange, red, pink, purple, and brown. In general, the dark-colored and pastel flowers need at least partial shade during the hottest part of the day to prevent them from fading or burning.

The floral color patterns include selfs (all perianth segments are the same color); bitones (the outer and inner segments differ in color intensity); bicolors (the outer and inner segments are different colors); blends of shades of a single color; eyed and banded (with distinct, contrasting color zones), and numerous other variations. The flowers vary in form from wide open and almost flat to funnel-shaped, trumpet-shaped, cuplike, triangular (with the outer perianth segments greatly recurved), spiders (long and narrow segments), and doubles. Recurved and ruffled perianth segments are found in many forms.

Most cultivars have been bred to produce many flowers (up to 50 or more per stalk). These flowers are more durable than those of the species, and bloom for a longer period of time. The flowers of some cultivars are fragrant.

The number of possible combinations of floral characteristics is almost limitless. New laboratory techniques creating tetraploids (plants with cells that have twice the normal number of chromosomes) promise even more variation. The proper choice of cultivar is the key to growing daylily hybrids successfully. Local growers, hybridizers, collectors, and nurserymen can provide information about cultivars that perform well in your region. The American Hemerocallis Society (ask your county Extension adviser for the address) is also a source of valuable information, and annually publishes a list of recommended cultivars selected by its members.

110

Hemerocallis lilioasphodelus

Lemon Daylily

Zone 3

Also known as Custard Lily, Lemon Lily,
Yellow Daylily

May be listed as *Hemerocallis flava, Hemerocallis lilioasphodelus* var. *flava*

Like the Tawny Daylily, the Lemon Daylily
has become naturalized throughout the eastern
United States. The plants are vigorous, spreading
by short to medium-long rhizomes that form
dense mounds of dark-green foliage about 2 feet
high. The leaves are up to 2 feet long by ¾ inch
wide. Texture is medium.

The lemon-yellow flowers are borne about
3 feet high on rather weak, nodding stalks. They
are 3 to 4 inches long, opening up to 3 to 4 inches
wide, and are agreeably fragrant. The flowers
open in the morning and often remain fresh into
the next day. (This desirable trait is called
"extended blooming.") Lemon Daylily is also the
earliest flowering species, blooming from late
May into June. The fruits are broadly elliptical
capsules about 1¾ inches long.

Lemon Daylily is somewhat more tolerant of
continuously moist soils than other daylily
species. It has been used extensively in hybridization because of its extended blooming and early
flowering date.

Hemerocallis lilioasphodelus 'Major' is taller
than the species, and has larger, deeper yellow
flowers.

Hosta species

Hosta

Liliaceae (Lily family)

Also known as Funkia, Plantain-Lily

May be listed as *Funkia* species

Hostas comprise a large group of hardy, dependable perennials that, when massed, are among the best ground covers for shaded locations. Their generally large, ribbed foliage creates bold, distinctive landscape effects. All of the leaves are basal, and arise from a compact crown that spreads very slowly by short rhizomes. The foliage forms neat, circular clumps of overlapping leaves. Some *Hosta* species may eventually spread to cover an area 4 to 5 feet square.

Although hostas are grown primarily for foliage effects, many species have the added attraction of showy, lilylike flowers. The flowers are borne on erect, leafless stalks that are usually much higher than the foliage mass. Hostas are deciduous, dying to the ground with the first autumn freeze. Spring regrowth is somewhat late. Texture for most hostas is medium-coarse to very coarse.

Leaves. Hostas have a wide variety of foliage forms. The leaves are petioled (often long-petioled), with very prominent, impressed, parallel veins that create a ribbed or puckered appearance. They are simple, entire, thick-textured to slightly fleshy, and range in size from only a few inches long to almost 1½ feet long. Leaf shapes vary from narrowly elliptic or egg-shaped to very broad or nearly rounded. Leaf colors range from bright green, to very dark green, to blue-green, to yellow-green. Many forms have foliage that is variegated with white or creamy yellow.

Flowers. Most hostas bloom in the summer. Certain species bloom as early as June or as late as September. The flowers are generally lavender-purple or lilac to almost white; one species has pure white flowers. A few forms have fragrant flowers, but most hostas have little or no fragrance.

The drooping or horizontally held flowers are borne in terminal, 1-sided racemes on erect, branchless, bracted stalks. Each flower has a short pedicel and a long perianth tube with 6 spreading lobes. The perianth tube may be gradually flaring and trumpetlike or abruptly enlarged and bell-shaped. The 6 stamens are as long as or slightly longer than the perianth. The stigma of the single, slender style usually protrudes beyond the corolla.

Culture. Hostas will grow in sun or shade in any moderately fertile, well-drained soil. They grow best in high, open shade (such as that provided by deciduous trees) in a moist soil that is rich in organic matter. If hostas are grown primarily for their foliage effects, they can be grown in dense shade where they will not flower well or may not flower at all. Hostas thrive in a cool, sunny location if the soil is kept moist. In sun and heat, they are subject to a loss of vigor, poor foliage color (especially the variegated foliage forms), and leaf burn. Do not plant in soggy, poorly drained soils.

Incorporate humus in the form of leaf mold, well-rotted compost, or rotted manure into the planting bed. An organic mulch may be beneficial until foliage cover is complete. After the plants are established, the foliage shades the ground so completely that weeds are eliminated and soil moisture is retained, making additional mulching unnecessary.

Water hostas during periods of drouth, and apply a complete fertilizer annually. Heavy, infrequent waterings are recommended. To preserve the best appearance of the plant and to prevent unwanted seedlings, remove the flower stalks after the flowers have faded. Named varieties and hybrids do not reproduce true to type from seed, and their seedlings can become a nuisance.

Hostas are most easily propagated by division in the spring or early fall. Small sections may be removed from very large plants without disturbing the entire plant. Although some *Hosta* species are sterile, many produce viable seeds. The seeds have no dormancy or chilling requirements, and germinate readily. Seedlings may produce mutants, however, and will not flower for 2 to 3 years.

Plant hostas in the spring or early fall. If planted in the fall, they need a protective mulch for the winter. Space plants 2 to 3 feet apart, depending upon the species planted. Hostas require little or no care after they are established.

These plants are generally untroubled by diseases. Slugs and chewing insects may sometimes damage foliage, and large-leaf forms in open sites may be subject to tatter from high winds.

Uses. Hostas are excellent ground covers for almost any degree of shade. They can be used effectively in both formal and informal landscapes, and are even suitable for wooded, naturalized areas. If hostas are planted in combination with spring flowering bulbs and other ephemerals, their lush foliage will mask the disappearance of these other plants. Mixed beds of hostas (small groupings of various species) create interesting contrasts in size and leaf color and shape. When hostas are planted closely together, their overlapping leaves will completely obscure the ground. A totally different effect can be achieved when certain *Hosta* species are widely spaced and combined with a mulch to emphasize the symmetry of each plant.

Hostas are valued for their bold, decorative foliage, dependability and persistence, and neat growth habits.

Most *Hosta* species are native to Japan. A few are native to China and Korea. Numerous hybrids and horticultural varieties are also available. The nomenclature of this large, botanically complex genus has been subject to frequent revision, resulting in great confusion in the nursery trade. Commercial growers often sell mislabeled plants, and the same plant may be offered under a wide variety of names. Read the plant descriptions carefully, and, whenever possible, see the plants before buying.

The genus *Hosta* was named to commemorate Nicolaus Thomas Host, the nineteenth-century Austrian physician and botanist. The common name "Plantain-Lily" probably arose from the similarity in appearance of hostas to the lawn weed *Plantago rugelii* (Blackseed Plantain). The American Hosta Society was founded to foster interest in these plants.

Hosta crispula

Whiterim Plantain-Lily

Zone 4

May be listed as *Hosta marginata*

Whiterim Plantain-Lily has oval, dark-green leaves that are about 9 inches long and irregularly margined with white. The wavy edged leaves are long-petioled, with 7 to 9 veins on each side of the midrib.

Whiterim Plantain-Lily flowers in July. The funnel-shaped, pale-lavender flowers are about 2 inches long, and are borne in loose racemes on stalks that grow 2 to 3 feet high. Seeds are produced abundantly. To prevent unwanted seedlings, remove the flower stalks after the flowers have faded.

(For other hostas with white-margined leaves, see *Hosta decorata, Hosta fortunei* 'Marginato-alba', page 115, and *Hosta sieboldii,* page 117.)

Hosta decorata

Blunt Plantain-Lily

Zone 3

May be listed as *Hosta* 'Thomas Hogg'

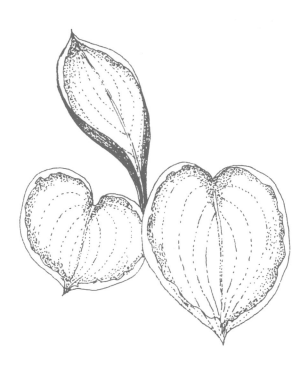

Blunt Plantain-Lily forms compact foliage mounds up to 1 foot high that spread by stolons. The dark-green leaves are about 6 inches long, and have an irregular white margin somewhat narrower than that of *Hosta crispula*. They are egg-shaped to elliptic, with 4 to 5 pairs of prominent, impressed veins. The leaf apex is usually blunt but may have a very short, abrupt point. Each leaf is borne on a long, winged petiole.

The dark-violet flowers are produced in August. They are 2 inches long, with a narrow bell-shaped perianth. The 2-foot-long flower stalks may have few to many flowers. Seeds are produced abundantly. To prevent unwanted seedlings, remove the flower stalks after the flowers have faded.

Hosta fortunei

Fortune's Plantain-Lily

Zone 3

Also known as Tall Cluster Plantain-Lily

Fortune's Plantain-Lily forms large clumps of foliage that grow to 1½ feet high and may spread to 5 feet in diameter. The pale-green leaves are 5 inches long and 3 inches wide, and have a grayish cast. They are egg-shaped (the base is often heart-shaped), with 8 to 10 pairs of prominent veins.

The pale-lilac to violet flowers are borne in July on stalks that are much higher than the foliage, growing to 3 feet high. The funnel-shaped perianth may be up to 1½ inches long.

Fortune's Plantain-Lily may be of hybrid origin, with *Hosta sieboldiana* (see page 116) one of the parents.

Hosta fortunei 'Marginato-alba' (may be listed as 'Albomarginata') has leaf blades up to 1 foot long that are broadly margined with white. This plant is very similar to *Hosta crispula*.

Hosta fortunei 'Aurea' has thin leaves that are yellowish when they emerge, turning light green by summer. 'Aureomaculata' also has thin leaves. The leaves are yellowish edged with a narrow band of green when they emerge, turning entirely green in the summer.

Hosta lancifolia

Narrow-leaved Plantain-Lily

Zone 3

Also known as Japanese Plantain-Lily

May be listed as *Hosta japonica*

For a color illustration of *Hosta lancifolia*, see page 68.

Narrow-leaved Plantain-Lily is one of the most satisfactory hostas for use as a ground cover. It is competitive with tree roots, and is more tolerant of dry conditions than other *Hosta* species. Its leaves grow thickly, forming large masses that completely obscure the ground. The foliage grows to about 1½ feet high, and a single plant may spread to 2 feet in diameter.

The glossy, green leaves are narrowly egg-shaped to elliptic. They are 5 to 7 inches long and 2½ to 3½ inches wide, with 5 to 6 veins on each side of the midrib and long, slender, purple-dotted petioles.

Narrow-leaved Plantain-Lily flowers from late August to early September. The flower stalks are 2 to 2½ feet high, with 2 to 5 green, leaflike bracts. From 5 to 30 well-spaced flowers occur on each stalk. The bell-shaped perianth is violet with whitish streaks, and is 1½ to 2 inches long and about 1 inch wide.

Hosta plantaginea

Fragrant Plantain-Lily

Zone 3

Also known as Assumption Lily, August Lily

May be listed as *Hosta grandiflora, Hosta subcordata*

Fragrant Plantain-Lily forms coarse mounds of foliage that reach 2 feet in height and spread to 3 feet wide. The petioled, glossy, yellowish green leaves may grow to 10 inches long and about 7 inches wide. They are broadly egg-shaped, with a rounded or somewhat heart-shaped base and 7 to 9 parallel veins on each side of the midrib.

The fragrant, waxy white flowers are borne in crowded, terminal racemes on bracted stalks that grow 2½ feet high. The horizontally held perianth is trumpet-shaped, flaring toward the apex, and may be 5 inches long and 2 to 3 inches in diameter. Each flower is subtended by 1 or more (usually 2) leafy bracts. Fragrant Plantain-Lily blooms from mid-August to mid-September, and its flowers are generally considered the most beautiful of the hostas.

Plant in the spring so that the roots have an entire season to develop; a good root system is essential to overwintering well. A protective mulch may be necessary the first winter.

A recommended cultivar is *Hosta plantaginea* 'Grandiflora'. This selection has longer leaves and longer, narrower flowers than the species.

Hosta sieboldiana

Siebold Plantain-Lily

Zone 3

Also known as Blue-Leaved Plantain-Lily

May be listed as *Hosta glauca*

Siebold Plantain-Lily is a large, imposing plant grown for its grayish blue-green, distinctly ribbed foliage. The clumps grow to 2½ feet high and spread to 3 feet in diameter. The rigid, thick leaves are covered with a whitish wax that gives them their unusual coloration. The leaves are large (10 to 15 inches long and 6 to 10 inches wide) and very broadly elliptic to egg-shaped, with a short-pointed apex. The crinkled, ribbed appearance of the foliage is created by 12 or more prominently impressed veins on each side of the midrib.

The flowers are produced on 2-foot-long stalks that are often hidden among the foliage. The very pale lilac flowers are borne from early July to August in 6 to 10 flowered, short, dense racemes.

Many cultivars are available commercially.

Hosta sieboldii

Seersucker Plantain-Lily

Zone 3

Also known as Whiterim Plantain-Lily

May be listed as *Hosta albomarginata, Hosta lancifolia albomarginata*

For a color illustration of *Hosta sieboldii*, see page 68.

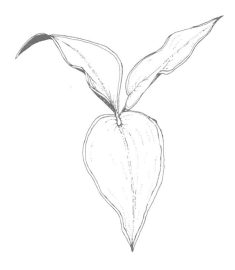

Seersucker Plantain-Lily forms clumps that spread to about 2 feet in diameter. The leaves and flowers are similar to those of *Hosta lancifolia* (see page115). The dark-green leaves are narrowly egg-shaped to elliptic, with a very thin marginal band of white or yellowish white. From 4 to 6 pairs of lateral veins give the leaves a puckered appearance.

The flowers are 1½ to 2 inches long, and are borne in late August and early September on stalks that grow 2 to 3 feet high. As many as 30 flowers may be produced on a single stalk. The trumpet-shaped perianth is violet with darker purple streaks. Seeds are produced abundantly. To prevent unwanted seedlings, remove the flower stalks after the flowers have faded.

Hosta sieboldii 'Alba' has white flowers and green leaves without white margins.

Hosta undulata

Wavy-leaved Plantain-Lily

Zone 3

May be listed as *Hosta lancifolia* var. *undulata*

Wavy-leaved Plantain-Lily is one of the smaller leaved hostas, forming mounds that are usually less than 20 inches wide. The leaves are about 6 inches long and 3 inches wide. They have an undulating margin and a broad, creamy yellow-to-white splash down the center. The leaf blade is elliptic to egg-shaped, with a sharp, pointed apex; the base is abruptly narrowed into a long, winged petiole. There are 10 pairs of lateral veins.

The trumpet-shaped, pale lavender flowers are about 2 inches long, and are borne in July on stalks that may grow to 3 feet high. Usually about 10 flowers are produced on a single stalk.

Although Wavy-leaved Plantain-Lily tolerates full sun better than many other *Hosta* species, it is less variegated when grown in the sun. It is used widely as an edging plant for perennial borders and walkways. Because the species is sterile, there are no unwanted seedlings.

Wavy-leaved Plantain-Lily is known only in cultivation, and is probably of hybrid origin. Its nomenclature is confused, and plants offered commercially as *Hosta variegata* and *Hosta medio-picta* are often *Hosta undulata*.

Hosta undulata 'Erromena' is slightly larger and more robust than the species. Its leaves are green and have less wavy margins than those of Wavy-leaved Plantain-Lily. This plant may also be listed as *Hosta erromena, Hosta lancifolia* var. *fortis,* and *Hosta undulata* var. *erromena.*

Hosta undulata 'Univittata' has leaves that have a narrow central stripe and are less wavy than those of the species.

Hosta ventricosa

Blue Plantain-Lily

Zone 3

Blue Plantain-Lily, as its name indicates, has flowers that are more nearly blue than those of any other *Hosta* species. The large, lustrous, dark-green leaves are very broadly egg-shaped or heart-shaped, with a slightly twisted, short-pointed apex. They may grow to 9 inches long and 8 inches wide. There are 7 to 9 parallel veins on each side of the midrib.

The dark-violet to almost blue flowers are borne in July, and are lifted well above the foliage on stems 3 feet long. The perianth tube is abruptly bell-shaped, and about 2 inches long. From 10 to 15 flowers occur per stalk. Seeds are produced abundantly. To prevent unwanted seedlings, remove the flower stalks after the flowers have faded.

Iberis sempervirens

Evergreen Candytuft

Zone 4

Brassicaceae or Cruciferae (Mustard family)

Also known as Edging Candytuft, Perennial Candytuft

For a color illustration of *Iberis sempervirens* 'Snowflake', see page 68.

Evergreen Candytuft forms a dense mound of glossy, dark-green foliage about 8 to 12 inches high and 2 feet in diameter. The spreading stems are decumbent (turn upward at their tips), and are often somewhat woody at the base. They root wherever they touch moist soil. For about 6 weeks in the spring, the foliage is almost completely hidden by a profusion of flowers. Growth rate is slow to medium. Texture is medium-fine.

Leaves. The small, thick, evergreen leaves are alternate, about ½ inch long, and smooth and glossy. They are narrow (about 1/10 to 1/8 inch wide), and have parallel, entire (untoothed) margins and a blunt apex.

Flowers. The bright, pure white flowers are borne abundantly from late April to mid-June in somewhat flattened racemes about 2 inches wide. Each flower consists of 4 spreading petals; the 2 petals toward the center of the inflorescence are smaller than the 2 outer petals. If the plants are allowed to form fruits, the racemes elongate as the fruits are produced.

Culture. Evergreen Candytuft will grow in light shade but will not flower as profusely as when grown in full sun. Any moist, moderately fertile soil is suitable as long as it is well drained. Incorporate 2 to 3 inches of decomposed organic matter into the planting bed. This plant is slow growing, and an organic mulch will help control weeds until the cover is complete.

Soggy winter soils decrease the hardiness of this plant. Evergreen Candytuft is also subject to tip burn and desiccation in northern climates where winter snow cover is not complete. If tip burning is not extensive, remove the browned stem tips by shearing lightly in early spring. When damage is more severe, a protective winter covering of evergreen boughs is recommended.

To encourage dense, compact growth, clip the plants almost halfway to the ground after they have flowered (if plants are not clipped, they become loose and open in the center). Applying a complete fertilizer after you have clipped the plants will promote vigorous growth. The only other maintenance required is watering during periods of dry weather. Once established, Evergreen Candytuft is long-lived and permanent.

Plant in the spring or early fall. Space the plants 15 to 18 inches apart.

Propagation is by seeds, division, and cuttings. Seedlings are subject to wide variation, and divisions do not always establish well. The most satisfactory method is to take cuttings after flowering. These cuttings root easily. To assure uniform offspring, select plants for cuttings that are similar in size, growth habit, and foliage color.

This plant is usually not seriously affected by insect pests or diseases, although clubroot may be a problem in poorly drained soils.

Uses. Evergreen Candytuft is best used as a relatively small-scale ground cover in sunny areas with a well-drained soil. It can also be used effectively in rock gardens, trailing over dry walls, and as an edging plant for the shrub border. This plant is valued for its glossy, evergreen foliage and brilliant, white flowers.

119

Iberis sempervirens is native to southern Europe. *Iberis* is derived from Iberia, the ancient name for Spain, where numerous species of this genus are native.

A recommended selection of Evergreen Candytuft is *Iberis sempervirens* 'Snowflake'. This vigorous form grows to about 6 inches high and spreads to 3 feet in diameter. Its dark-green leaves are longer and broader than those of the species, and its white flowers are larger and are produced in larger clusters. Numerous dwarf, more compact forms of this cultivar are also available, but they are usually too small to be suitable for use as ground covers.

Lamiastrum galeobdolon 'Variegatum'

Yellow Archangel

Zone 4

Lamiaceae or Labiatae (Mint family)

Also known as Golden Dead Nettle, Silver
Frosted Dead Nettle, Silver Nettle Vine

May be listed as *Lamium galeobdolon,
Lamium galeobdolon* 'Variegatum'

For a color illustration of *Lamiastrum galeobdolon*
'Variegatum', see page 68.

Yellow Archangel is a deciduous, trailing, vinelike ground cover that forms sprawling mounds of foliage 1 to 1½ feet high. It spreads rapidly in all directions, and the stems root as they spread. Texture is medium-coarse.

Leaves. The leaves are opposite, and are borne on square stems. They are petioled and 1½ to 3 inches long; the upper surface is crinkly, with silver blotches between the veins that spread almost to the margins. The leaves are somewhat heart-shaped to almost rounded, with a rather blunt-pointed apex. The leaf margins are coarsely serrate, and the teeth are rounded. The foliage persists until temperatures become severe. Portions of the plant may sometimes revert to the green-leaved species. (The green-leaved species is too vigorous and invasive for use anywhere except in wild or naturalized plantings, and is widely cultivated.)

Flowers. The complete flowers are bright yellow with brownish markings. They are borne from mid-May through June on somewhat erect, leafy stems, and are clustered in the upper leaf axils. The lower portion of the 1-inch-long corolla is tubular; the upper portion is divided into an arched or hooded upper lip and a 3-lobed and drooping lower lip.

Culture. Yellow Archangel requires little care, and adapts to almost any area. It is best suited to shade and moist soil, but will grow in full sun if the soil is not allowed to become excessively dry. It is tolerant of poorer soils, where its vigorous growth can most easily be controlled.

Shearing in midsummer encourages more compact growth. The plant's spread is easily controlled by cutting back stems that grow out of bounds. If the plant escapes into lawn areas, it can be controlled with broadleaf lawn herbicides (ask your county Extension adviser for recommendations).

Propagation is by cuttings and division in early spring. Division is the easiest method. Space divisions (or purchased plants) 2 to 3 feet apart in the spring.

Uses. Yellow Archangel is best used as a ground cover in the shade, where its silver-marked foliage brightens shaded areas and contrasts pleasingly with darker foliaged plants. It is also an excellent ground cover in areas where its spread may be easily contained, such as between a sidewalk and building. This plant is sometimes used in hanging baskets as a houseplant.

Lamiastrum galeobdolon is native to woodlands and other shady sites from western Europe to Iran. Yellow Archangel has long been included in the genus *Lamium* (the suffix *-astrum* of the new genus name means "somewhat resembling"). It is now separated from the genus *Lamium* by its hairless anthers and by the lower lip of the corolla having 3 lobes of almost equal size. *Lamium* species usually have hairy anthers, and the middle lobe of the lower corolla lip is much larger than the 2 toothlike lateral lobes.

Lamium maculatum (Spotted Dead Nettle) is a closely related species that is an equally desirable ground cover. It is quite similar to

Yellow Archangel in its growth habit, cultural requirements, and uses. Its foliage is also marked with silver, but the silvery splotch is on the midvein and the leaf is slightly more narrow. The rose-purple flowers are produced from May to midsummer, and are much showier than those of Yellow Archangel. Because Spotted Dead Nettle tends to clump rather than spread, the plants should be spaced closer together than those of Yellow Archangel. Available cultivars include 'Album', a white flowering form; 'Aureum', which has leaves marked with yellow instead of silver; and 'Chequers', which has bluish violet flowers and silvery white leaves with only a narrow green margin.

Lathyrus latifolius

Perennial Pea

Zone 3

Fabaceae or Leguminosae (Pea family)

Also known as Everlasting Pea, Perennial Pea Vine, Sweet Pea

For a color illustration of *Lathyrus latifolius*, see page 69.

Perennial Pea is a grayish green, scrambling, deciduous vine that mounds upon itself or climbs by twining tendrils. The stems rapidly grow 6 to 9 feet long from a relatively static, large, fleshy root system. The showy flowers are produced throughout the summer months. Texture is medium-coarse.

Leaves. The leaves are borne alternately along broadly winged stems. Each leaf is composed of a single pair of narrowly to broadly elliptical or egg-shaped leaflets that may be up to 4 inches long, with a small, sharp, very abrupt point at the apex. Stout, branching tendrils arise between the leaflet pairs, and there are 2 large, leaflike stipules at the base of the winged petiole.

Flowers. Perennial Pea has a very long flowering period (usually from late June through August). The attractive, pealike flowers vary in color from pale pink to deep rosy purple and white. They are 1 to 1½ inches wide, and are borne in racemes on long, axillary peduncles that reach above the foliage.

Culture. Perennial Pea grows best in full sun and in a well-drained soil, although it will grow well in nearly any soil and is tolerant of most exposures. This plant is extremely long-lived and easy to care for. Water the plants or seedlings until they are established. Once established, Perennial Pea survives neglect, and is even difficult to eradicate if that should become necessary. Removing faded flowers will extend the flowering period and eliminate seeds. This plant may self-sow invasively.

Propagation is by seeds or division of clumps in the spring. Seeds sown in early spring will germinate in 2 to 3 weeks. Space divisions, seedlings, or purchased plants 1½ to 2 feet apart for a dense cover.

Perennial Pea is not usually affected seriously by insects or diseases, but downy mildew, anthracnose, root rots, and aphids may be troublesome. Aphids are probably the most common and destructive pest of this plant. Ask your county Extension adviser for control recommendations.

Uses. Perennial Pea is not a suitable plant for a refined landscape. It is best used as a cover for wild, rough areas and rocky slopes or to conceal fences and trellises.

Lathyrus latifolius is native to Europe, and has become widely naturalized in the United States.

A recommended cultivar is *Lathyrus latifolius* 'Splendens', which has very dark-purple to red flowers. 'Albus' is a white-flowering form.

Liriope spicata

Lilyturf

Zone 4

Liliaceae (Lily family)

Also known as Creeping Lilyturf, Liriope

For a color illustration of *Liriope spicata*, see page 69.

Lilyturf forms dense mats of narrow, grasslike foliage about 10 inches high. The foliage turns an unattractive straw color during the winter in northern climates. The flowers are borne in spikes that rise just above the foliage mass. Growth rate is moderate to rapid, the plants spreading by short rhizomes. Texture is fine to medium-fine.

Leaves. The medium- to deep-green, arching, grasslike leaves are stemless, up to 1½ feet long, and less than ½ inch wide. The leaf margins are finely serrate, with small, translucent teeth.

Flowers. The perfect, symmetrical flowers are ¼ inch in diameter, and are borne from mid-July to early September. The flower spikes resemble those of the Grape-hyacinth (*Muscari botryoides*), and range in color from light lilac to almost white. The erect, flowering stalk is light violet-brown, becoming violet toward its apex.

Fruits. The persistent, berrylike, fleshy, black fruits are produced in the fall.

Culture. Lilyturf is tolerant of the widest range of light conditions, from full sun to deep shade. Although this plant can adapt to almost any soil, it grows best in a moist, well-drained, moderately fertile soil. When Lilyturf is grow in the shade, the foliage is a darker green. In full shade, growth may be somewhat slowed and flowering considerably reduced.

Lilyturf requires little care. Mow or cut off old foliage close to the ground before regrowth starts in early spring. Although established plantings in full sun are quite tolerant of heat and drouth, a thorough, deep watering is beneficial during prolonged dry periods. After 4 to 5 years, it may be necessary to thin the planting to reduce overcrowding and maintain vigor.

Propagation is by division in early spring. Space divisions (or purchased plants) 1 foot apart in the spring.

Uses. Lilyturf is most often used as a border or edging plant, but it is an excellent ground cover for almost any location. Its grasslike foliage creates a unique textural effect. Do not plant in areas with foot traffic.

Liriope spicata is native to China, Japan, and Vietnam.

Liriope muscari (Big Blue Lilyturf, Mondo Grass) is a related species. It is slightly larger and showier than Lilyturf, and remains evergreen in the lower portions of Zone 6. Mondo Grass grows 1½ to 2 feet high, and its leaves are up to 2 feet long and ¾ inch wide. The dark-violet flowers are borne above the foliage. Unfortunately, this plant is often sold interchangeably with *Liriope spicata*. A more southern species, *Liriope muscari* is hardy only to Zone 6.

Orphiopogon japonicus, which is hardy only to Zone 7, is another related species that is frequently confused with *Liriope spicata*. The flowers of this plant, unlike those of Lilyturf, are borne below the foliage.

124

Lotus corniculatus

Birdsfoot Trefoil

Zone 3

Fabaceae or Leguminosae (Pea family)

Also known as Baby's Slippers, Bacon and Eggs, Birdsfoot Deervetch, Ground Honeysuckle

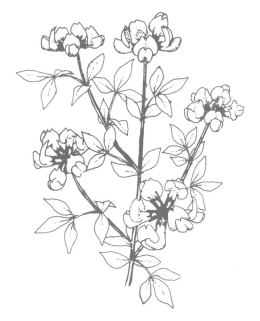

Birdsfoot Trefoil is a tough, durable, deciduous ground-cover plant that forms large, dense mounds of erect to trailing stems 1 to 2 feet high. The plants spread rapidly, growing to 2½ feet or more in diameter. They also self-sow readily. The bright, emerald-green foliage is usually covered with yellow flowers throughout the summer months. Texture is medium-fine.

Leaves. The pinnately compound leaves are borne alternately along the stems. They are composed of 3 cloverlike, egg-shaped to narrowly egg-shaped leaflets. The 2 large stipules at the base of the petiole resemble the leaflets so closely that some authorities contend that Birdsfoot Trefoil leaves have 5 leaflets.

Flowers. The small, pealike flowers are produced from June to September. They are a vivid, deep yellow (sometimes red tinged), and are borne singly or in umbels of 3 to 6 flowers on long, axillary peduncles.

Fruits. The fruits of Birdsfoot Trefoil are slender pods about 1 inch long. They are held in a 3-pronged arrangement resembling a bird's foot, giving the common name to this plant.

Culture. Birdsfoot Trefoil is a rugged plant that is most suited to poor soils in full sun. It is adapted to a wide pH range, thriving in soil with a pH from 4.5 to 8.0. This plant has a deep, branching root system that makes it quite drouth-tolerant. It is also tolerant of heat and light shade. In fertile soils, Birdsfoot Trefoil becomes almost shrublike and may spread invasively.

Plantings are somewhat slow in becoming established, and small plants and seedlings do not tolerate competition from weeds. For best results, keep the plants moist and weeded until they are well established. Once established, Birdsfoot Trefoil may be mowed regularly. It does not require mowing as often as a lawn, and may be used as a turfgrass substitute for rough areas. Set mower blades at least 6 inches high.

Propagation is by seeds sown at the rate of 2 pounds per 1,000 square feet. The seeds, like those of other legumes, should be inoculated with nitrogen-fixing bacteria. Birdsfoot Trefoil may also be propagated by division and cuttings. Space plants 1 foot apart.

Uses. Birdsfoot Trefoil is often grown along highway embankments. In combination with perennial grasses (tall fescue, bromegrass, and Kentucky bluegrass), it is an effective erosion control. This plant is used most effectively in large, rough, or wild, sunbaked locations; it is not suitable for small or refined landscape areas. Birdsfoot Trefoil is sometimes grown as a forage crop.

Lotus corniculatus is native to Europe and Asia, and has become widely naturalized throughout the northeastern and midwestern United States. The aquatic plants commonly known as Lotus belong to the unrelated genus *Nelumbo.*

Several strains of Birdsfoot Trefoil are available commercially. They vary in growth habit, height, flower color, and site tolerance. There is also an attractive, double-flowering form that may be listed as *Lotus corniculatus* var. *florepleno* or as the cultivar *Lotus corniculatus* 'Pleniflorus'.

Lysimachia nummularia

Moneywort

Zone 3

Primulaceae (Primrose family)

Also known as Creeping Charlie, Creeping Jenny

Moneywort is a trailing plant that sends out stems up to 2 feet long that root along their length at the nodes. It spreads rapidly to form ground-hugging, ruffled mats only 2 to 3 inches high. The bright green foliage, although not evergreen, usually persists until about December. In summer, the plants are dotted with golden yellow flowers. Texture is fine to medium-fine.

Leaves. The flat, shiny, almost circular leaves resemble small coins attached to the creeping stems. They are opposite, entire (without serrations), glabrous (smooth), and about 1 inch long, with petioles ½ to 1 inch long. The leaves are dotted with tiny black glands.

Flowers. The bright yellow, symmetrical, complete flowers are ¾ to 1 inch in diameter, and are borne on erect peduncles that arise from the leaf axils. The calyx has 5 or 6 sharp pointed lobes, and is ½ as long as the corolla; the 5 showy petals are oval, and are sparsely dotted with minute, dark glands. The flowers are borne in June and then sporadically throughout the summer.

Culture. Moneywort is an adaptable plant that requires little care. It grows best in the shade in moist to wet soils with added organic matter; it will, however, grow in the sun if the soil is kept sufficiently moist. This plant does not grow well in dry soils.

When Moneywort is grown in locations for which it is well suited, it may become weedy and need to be restrained. The creeping stems are easily uprooted, and invasions into lawn areas can be controlled with a broadleaf lawn herbicide.

Moneywort should be watered during periods of drouth. When grown in poor soils, it benefits from the application of a complete fertilizer each spring; otherwise, fertilization is necessary only when the plants show a decline in vigor.

Propagation is by seeds sown in the spring or by separation of the rooted stem segments at any time during the growing season. Space plants 15 to 18 inches apart.

Moneywort is not seriously affected by insect pests or diseases.

Uses. This plant grows well beneath trees in moist, densely shaded areas where its bright green foliage and yellow flowers provide a pleasing contrast. It can also be used effectively in wet soils beside streams and ponds and between paving and stepping-stones. Because Moneywort spreads vigorously, it should be used in naturalized areas where its spread does not need to be restricted, in areas where its spread is limited by adjacent dry, sunny areas, or in areas where it can easily be kept in bounds.

Lysimachia nummularia is native to Europe, but has become widely naturalized throughout northeastern North America.

An available selection is the cultivar *Lysimachia nummularia* 'Aurea', a yellow-foliage form. It is not as vigorous as the species, and requires a moist soil and full sun for best foliage coloration.

Nepeta × *faassenii*

Catmint

Zone 4

Lamiaceae or Labiatae (Mint family)

Also known as Mauve Catmint, Persian Catmint, Persian Ground-ivy

May be listed as *Nepeta mussinii, Nepeta
pseudomussinii*

For a color illustration of *Nepeta* × *faassenii*, see
page 69.

Catmint forms airy mounds of soft, gray,
deciduous foliage that grow 1 to 1½ feet high
and spread to about 1½ feet wide. The flowers
are borne in loose terminal clusters. When in
flower, the plants are about 2 feet high. The
showy flowers are attractive for a long period
of time. The rate of spread is moderate to rapid.
Texture is medium-fine.

Leaves. The aromatic leaves are opposite (each
pair is at right angles to the next, on erect, square
stems), about 1½ inches long, and narrowly
egg-shaped; the leaf surface is crinkled, and the
margin is serrate, with rounded serrations. The
leaves and stems are covered with a thick, short,
whitish pubescence.

Flowers. Catmint flowers from late May through
July, and then intermittently until September.
The abundant, asymmetrical, violet-blue flowers
are borne in axillary cymes toward the apices
of the stems. The tubular, pubescent calyx is
about ½ as long as the corolla. The corolla is
up to ½ inch long and 2-lipped (the upper lip
is 2-lobed and erect, and the lower lip is 3-lobed
and spreading). This hybrid is sterile, and does
not produce fruit.

Culture. Catmint grows best in full sun.
Almost any well-drained soil is suitable. Incorporate a complete fertilizer into the planting
bed, and water periodically to ensure rapid
coverage. Once the planting is established, it
can tolerate both heat and drouth.

After the first flowers have faded, cut back the
stems to ⅓ to ½ their original length. Removing
all of these flowers will produce vigorous new
growth and a bushier habit, and may result in
a second heavy flowering in late summer. If
the dead, unsightly flowers are not removed,

flowering is sparse throughout the remainder
of the summer.

A light mulch may be necessary in areas with
severe winter weather. Dead plant stems and
leaves can be allowed to remain for additional
protection; these should be removed along with
the mulch in very early spring before regrowth
begins.

Catmint is most easily propagated by division
in the spring. It may also be propagated by stem
cuttings taken of the new growth produced
after the plants were cut back following flowering.
Plant in the spring. Space plants 1 to 1½ feet apart.

This plant is generally pest free, although rust
may be a problem during particularly wet summers
or if the soil is poorly drained.

Uses. Catmint is often used as an edging or
border plant and in rock gardens. When massed,
it is an excellent ground cover for dry slopes and
other hot, sunny locations. This plant is as
attractive to cats as catnip (*Nepeta cataria*),
and they enjoy rolling in it. (This fact may be worth
considering if you are concerned about keeping
the planting neat.) Catmint is valued for its
profuse flowering and long period of bloom,
and for its soft, hazy foliage effect.

Nepeta × *faassenii* originated before 1939 in the
Copenhagen Botanic Gardens, Denmark, and is
the result of a cross between *Nepeta mussinii*
and *Nepeta nepetella*. It is often sold commercially
as *Nepeta mussinii*. An inferior plant, *Nepeta
mussinii* may be distinguished from Catmint by
its sprawling habit (the prostrate stems are 1 foot
long and curve upwards at their apices); its less
pubescent, grayish green foliage; and its shorter
blooming period.

Pachysandra procumbens

Allegany Pachysandra

Zone 4

Buxaceae (Boxwood family)

Also known as Allegany Spurge, Mountain Pachysandra, Mountain Spurge

For a color illustration of *Pachysandra procumbens*, see page 69.

Allegany Pachsandra is a little-known relative of the widely cultivated *Pachysandra terminalis* (Japanese Pachysandra). It forms broad, slowly spreading clumps of deciduous to semievergreen foliage that grow 8 to 10 inches high. The flowers are borne in very early spring before regrowth begins. Texture is medium.

Leaves. The leathery, grayish to bluish green leaves are alternate, but they are so closely clustered towards the apices of the stems that they appear whorled. The leaves are 2 to 3½ inches long and broadly rounded, with large, coarse serrations on the upper ½ of the leaf margin. The base of the leaf is narrowed to form a petiole. The foliage becomes somewhat bronzish in late fall, and (although often flattened to the ground by the weather), usually persists in a semievergreen condition throughout the winter. In exposed northern locations without winter snow cover, Allegany Pachysandra is deciduous and dies to the ground.

Flowers. Allegany Pachysandra may flower from late March until May. Flowering starts before the foliage begins regrowth. The pinkish to purplish white flowers are borne in erect, short spikes that arise from the base of the stems. They are unisexual and without petals. The male flowers are borne at the tops of the spikes, and the few female flowers are borne at the bases. Although not particularly ornamental, the flowers are significant because of their early flowering date. They are also fragrant and highly attractive to bees. In severe winter climates where Allegany Pachysandra is deciduous, the flowers will be killed by the weather.

Fruits. The fruits are 3-valved capsules that are seldom produced in cultivation.

Culture. Allegany Pachysandra grows best in a moist, well-drained, humus-rich soil that is slightly acidic to neutral (pH from 5 to 7). It should be grown in areas with ½ to full shade.

Incorporate peat moss, well-rotted leaf mold, or compost into the planting bed and also apply as a mulch 1 to 2 inches deep. The incorporated organic matter not only adds nutrients to the soil but improves the soil structure, facilitating the spread of the clumps. Mulch helps conserve soil moisture and controls weeds until the clumps have merged.

Keep the planting moist until it is well established. Add about 1 inch of mulch each spring until the cover is complete and apply a complete fertilizer at the same time. Plantings of Allegany Pachysandra are virtually permanent, and may be left undisturbed indefinitely.

Propagation is by division of the clumps in early spring or by cuttings taken in early summer after growth has matured. Cuttings root readily, and are a more satisfactory means of propagation than clump division. Plant the cuttings 8 to 10 inches apart in late summer after a vigorous root system has developed.

Unlike Japanese Pachysandra, Allegany Pachysandra is not seriously affected by insect pests or diseases.

Uses. Allegany Pachysandra is an excellent ground cover for use in the shade beneath trees and shrubs. It is valued for its bluish or grayish green foliage.

Pachysandra procumbens is native to woodlands from West Virginia south to Florida and west to Kentucky and Mississippi.

128

Phalaris arundinacea var. *picta*

Ribbon Grass

Zone 3

Poaceae or Graminae (Grass family)

Also known as Gardener's Garters

May be listed as *Phalaris arundinacea* 'Picta'

For a color illustration of *Phalaris arundinacea* var. *picta*, see page 70.

Ribbon Grass is a deciduous, ornamental grass that has been long cultivated for its decorative striped foliage. It spreads rapidly by rhizomes to form upright, open masses of foliage that somewhat resemble bamboo. It usually grows 2 to 3 feet high, but may grow to 5 feet high. Texture is medium.

Leaves. The flat leaves are 6 to 12 inches long and ½ to ¾ inch wide. They are medium green and longitudinally striped with white, yellow, or (occasionally) pink. When Ribbon Grass is grown in a dry location, the lower leaves become brown and unattractive by late August.

Flowers. The white to buff flowers are borne from early June to mid-July in panicles 4 to 6 inches long. They are not ornamental.

Culture. Ribbon Grass should be grown in full sun (where its growth is densest) or light shade. This plant is tolerant of wet or dry sites, and grows best in an infertile, sandy or heavy clay soil. When planted in a fertile loam, Ribbon Grass grows too high, the leaves may lose their variegation, and the spread may be so vigorous that the planting becomes loose and open.

The foliage dies to the ground with the first heavy frost in the autumn. Mow or clip the dry remains before regrowth starts in early spring. This rugged, durable plant does not require special care. Mowing at any time during the growing season encourages denser growth and helps keep the planting within bounds.

Propagation is by division of the rhizomes in the spring. Space divisions 1 to 2 feet apart.

Ribbon Grass is not seriously affected by insect pests or diseases.

Uses. This plant should be used where little else will grow, or in areas where its spread can be easily controlled. It is especially effective as an erosion control on dry, sunny slopes and along stream banks. Ribbon Grass is valued for its interesting textural effect and bright color contrast.

Phalaris arundinacea var. *picta* is native to temperate North America and Europe.

Phlox subulata

Moss Pink

Zone 2

Polemoniaceae (Phlox family)

Also known as Creeping Phlox, Flowering Moss, Ground Pink, Moss Phlox, Mountain Pink

For a color illustration of *Phlox subulata*, see page 69.

Moss Pink is a low, mosslike, evergreen to semievergreen ground cover that grows to about 4 inches high (6 inches high in flower). It spreads rapidly by creeping stems that root along their lengths to form dense mats up to 2 feet in diameter. The masses of flowers almost completely conceal the foliage in the spring. Texture is fine.

Leaves. The simple, needlelike leaves are about 1 inch long, sharp-pointed, stiff, and prickly to the touch. They are very closely set, and are borne on stems that may become somewhat woody. The leaves are usually opposite, but the upper stem leaves may be alternate.

Flowers. The flowers are effective for nearly 4 weeks during April and May. There are various color forms, ranging from red-purple to violet-purple, pink, and white. Many selections have been made for superior flower color. The symmetrical, bisexual flowers are borne in profuse clusters on short, flowering branches. Each flower has a 5-toothed calyx and a corolla with a narrow tube, 5 spreading, shallowly notched lobes, and 5 stamens. The corolla is about ¾ inch wide.

Culture. Moss Pink is a sturdy plant that can be grown easily in full sun in almost any well-drained soil. It grows best in gritty, slightly acid to slightly alkaline soils (pH of 6 to 8).

To encourage dense, more compact growth, cut the plants back halfway to the ground after flowering. Use a mower if the planting is large. Although Moss Pink is relatively tolerant of dry conditions, it has a shallow root system, and should be watered occasionally in dry weather.

Propagation is easiest by division in the spring after the flowers have faded. Only nonwoody divisions should be replanted. These must be cut back halfway to lessen the demands on the sparse root system. Space plants 10 to 12 inches apart. Keep the planting weeded and watered until it is well established.

Moss Pink is susceptible to attack by red spider mites during periods of hot, dry weather. Frequent waterings may help to alleviate this problem. Ask your county Extension adviser for appropriate chemical controls.

Uses. Moss Pink is a common rock-garden plant, and is often used as a trailing plant on walls. It is an excellent ground cover for sunny slopes and other well-drained locations in full sun. Mixed plantings that combine selections with various flower colors can be quite striking. Moss Pink is valued for its ground-hugging, dense foliage and its abundant, brilliant, prolonged flowering.

Phlox subulata is native to rocky slopes and sandy areas from New York to North Carolina and westward to Michigan.

The many selections of *Phlox subulata* with superior flower color include 'Alexander's Beauty', 'Alexander's Surprise', and 'Chuckles' (pink flowers); 'White Delight' (white flowers); and 'Red Wings' and 'Scarlet Flame' (red flowers).

Phlox nivalis (Trailing Phlox) is a related species that is sometimes confused with Moss Pink. This plant has long, prostrate stems that turn upward at their apices, and that bear awl-shaped,

130

evergreen leaves up to ½ inch long. The flowers are 1 inch wide, and vary in color from purple to pink to white. They are borne in cymes on more or less erect, flowering branches that hold the flowers just above the foliage. The lobes of the corolla may be entire, with an irregular margin, or with a shallow notch at the apex. Trailing Phlox may be distinguished from Moss Pink by its looser, more open habit and time of flowering. (The flowers of Trailing Phlox bloom in June and often bloom again in September.) The cultural requirements and uses of this plant are the same as those described for Moss Pink. *Phlox nivalis* is native from Virginia to Florida and Alabama. It is hardy to Zone 4. The cultivar 'Camla', which has salmon-pink flowers, is a recommended selection.

Phlox × procumbens (also commonly known as Trailing Phlox) is a hybrid of *Phlox stolonifera* and *Phlox subulata*. It grows best in dry soils in sun or light shade. Although this plant is quite similar to Moss Pink, it is somewhat shorter (3 to 5 inches high) and has broader, elliptic leaves. It produces masses of bright, rosy purple flowers from late April to late May, and is hardy to Zone 4.

Another related species is *Phlox stolonifera* (Creeping Phlox). It is larger and coarser than Moss Pink (growing 6 to 8 inches high), and has almost rounded, evergreen leaves that are 3½ inches long and have trailing stems. The purple-to-violet flowers are 1 inch wide, and are borne profusely in loose cymes on erect stems in April and May. A woodland plant, Creeping Phlox requires partial shade and a moist, somewhat

acid (pH 5 to 7), humus-rich soil. It cannot survive long periods of drouth without supplemental watering. Propagation is by division in early spring. This plant can be used effectively as a ground cover for large, rocky areas and shaded slopes. The cultivar 'Blue Ridge', which has clear, light-blue flowers, is a recommended selection.

Polygonum cuspidatum var. *compactum*

Low Japanese Fleeceflower

Zone 4

Polygonaceae (Smartweed family)

Also known as Dwarf Fleeceflower, Dwarf
Lace Plant, Dwarf Polygonum, Japanese
Knotweed, Reynoutria Fleeceflower

May be listed as *Polygonum compactum*,
Polygonum reynoutria

For color illustrations of *Polygonum cuspidatum* var.
compactum and *Polygonum bistorta*, see page 70.

Low Japanese Fleeceflower is a vigorous,
deciduous ground cover that forms large masses
as it grows. It reaches 1 to 2 feet in height,
and spreads so rapidly by rhizomes that it may
be invasive, especially in smaller locations.
This colorful plant has new spring foliage
marked with reddish bronze, red flower buds
that open to pinkish flowers, pink to red fruits,
and often brilliant red fall color. It dies to the
ground with the first hard frost. Texture is
medium-coarse.

Leaves. The leaves are simple and entire, and
are borne alternately on stout stems that are
swollen at the nodes, appearing jointed. A
stipular growth, the *ochrea* (characteristic of
this family), surrounds the stem at the base of
each petiole. The broadly oval to rounded leaves
are 3 to 6 inches long, with a short, abruptly
pointed apex and wavy margin. The petiole is
about 1 inch long.

Flowers. The small flowers are borne in dense,
axillary, panicled racemes in late August. The
pink to red buds open white to pink. Each
bisexual, petalless flower has 5 sepals and 8
stamens. The flowers create a delicate, lacy effect.

Fruits. The fruits are very showy, pink-to-red,
winged achenes that are effective from early
September until the first hard frost.

Culture. Low Japanese Fleeceflower establishes
itself easily and requires little care. It grows best
in full sun, and tolerates almost any soil,
including poor, dry, gravelly soils that help
restrict its vigorous spread.

The remains of the previous season's growth
should be cut off close to the ground before regrowth starts in the spring. Shear the planting
3 or 4 times during the growing season to obtain
a lower, denser habit.

Low Japanese Fleeceflower is most easily
propagated by division in the spring. Space
plants 1½ to 2 feet apart.

This plant is not seriously affected by insect
pests or diseases.

Uses. Low Japanese Fleeceflower is best
used to create bold effects in large areas where a
lower, more delicate ground cover would be
ineffective. Its vigorous root system also helps
control erosion on steep, sunny banks. This
plant is valued for its colorful foliage, flowers,
and fruits.

Polygonum cuspidatum var. *compactum* is native
to Japan.

Polygonum affine (Himalayan Fleeceflower) is a related species that is not as robust as Low Japanese Fleeceflower. Himalayan Fleeceflower is a "carpeting" plant that spreads above the ground, rooting at it spreads. The mostly basal, semievergreen leaves are narrowly oblong and 2 to 4 inches long. The tiny, rose-pink flowers are borne in 3-inch-long, dense, erect, terminal spikes on sparsely leafy stalks that grow to 1½ feet high. The flowers are effective from late August to early September. The fall foliage is russet red. Himalayan Fleeceflower grows in full sun to partial shade in almost any soil. Its spread is more easily controlled than that of the Low Japanese Fleeceflower, and this plant can be used in smaller areas where less tolerant ground covers will not grow. Propagation is by division. *Polygonum affine* is native to the Himalayas. It is hardy to Zone 3.

Polygonum bistorta (Snakeweed) is another related species that is becoming more widely available. The narrowly oval leaves, like those of Himalayan Fleeceflower, are mostly basal. The pink or white flowers are borne in dense, cylindrical, 1- to 2-inch-long, terminal spikes on stalks 1½ to 2 feet high. If given adequate moisture, Snakeweed will flower from May through July. This clump-forming plant grows best in a moist, fertile soil in partial shade. Propagation is by division. The cultivar *Polygonum bistorta* 'Superbum' is a better ground-cover plant than Snakeweed. It grows 2 to 3 feet high and flowers more profusely than the species. *Polygonum bistorta* is native to northern Europe and Asia. It is hardy to Zone 4.

Potentilla tabernaemontani

Potentilla verna

Zone 3

Rosaceae (Rose family)

Also known as Spring Cinquefoil

For a color illustration of *Potentilla tabernaemontani*, see page 70.

Potentilla verna is a somewhat hairy, deciduous to semievergreen ground cover that forms compact, low-growing mats 3 to 6 inches high. It is a variable species, usually spreading by prostrate, rooting stems. These stems have short, ascending branches, and may grow up to 20 inches long. The base of the plant becomes woody and persistent with age. The bright-yellow flowers are borne profusely above the foliage mats in the spring. Growth rate is medium to rapid. Texture is fine.

Leaves. The rich-green leaves are alternate, and are palmately divided into 5 (sometimes 7) leaflets. The narrowly oval to egg-shaped leaflets are sessile or very short-stalked. They may be up to 1½ inches long and ½ inch wide, but are usually smaller. The leaflet margins are coarsely toothed.

Flowers. Potentilla verna flowers during May and June, and sometimes sparsely in August or September. The complete flowers are ½ to nearly 1 inch wide, and are borne singly or in terminal cymes. Each flower is subtended by 5 tiny bracts that are shorter than the 5 sepals. The 5 showy petals are bright golden yellow.

Culture. This plant grows well in almost any well-drained, not extremely fertile soil that is neutral to alkaline, and is tolerant of slightly acidic soils. It tolerates full sun but grows best in partial shade. Although somewhat tolerant of drouth, Potentilla verna should be watered during dry periods. When necessary, fertilize in early spring, and cut the plants back whenever they become unkempt.

Potentilla verna is most easily propagated by division of rootstocks in early spring. It may also be grown from seeds sown in sandy soil and overwintered in a cold frame. Plant in early spring. Space plants 1 foot apart.

This plant is not seriously affected by insects or diseases. It is valued for its attractive flowers and low, dense growth habit, and is readily available commercially.

Uses. Potentilla verna can be used effectively in rock gardens and to cover small slopes and open areas in partial shade. Because this species varies considerably, it is wise to see the plants before purchasing.

Potentilla tabernaemontani is native to Europe and western Asia.

Potentilla tridentata

Wineleaf Cinquefoil

Zone 3

Rosaceae (Rose family)

Also known as Threetoothed Cinquefoil

Wineleaf Cinquefoil is a low-growing, mat-forming, evergreen ground cover that grows 4 to 10 inches high and spreads by underground stems. The base of the stems is woody. Growth rate is fast.

Leaves. The evergreen leaves are palmately compound, with 3 leaflets from ½ to 2 inches long. Each leaflet is narrowly oval-shaped and has 3 (occasionally 5) teeth at the apex and a wedge-shaped base. The leaves are leathery and glossy dark-green in the summer; in the fall, the upper (youngest) leaves remain green, while the leaves immediately beneath them turn wine red. The oldest (lowest) leaves turn yellow and drop.

Flowers. The white flowers are borne above the leaves in few- to many-flowered clusters. They have 5 petals, are ¼ inch wide, and are not as showy as those of Potentilla verna.

Fruits. The fruits are hairy achenes that are not ornamental.

Culture. Wineleaf Cinquefoil requires a very acidic (pH below 5.0), well-drained soil. It is native to rocky, sandy areas, and will tolerate dry periods after it is established. This plant is salt tolerant. It grows best in partial shade but will tolerate full sun.

Propagation is by seeds, cuttings, and divisions. Space plants 6 to 12 inches apart.

This plant is not seriously affected by insects or diseases.

Uses. Wineleaf Cinquefoil is suitable for use in rock gardens and to cover open, rocky areas in partial shade.

Potentilla tridentata is native from Greenland to Manitoba and south to Georgia and Iowa. It was introduced in 1787.

Pulmonaria saccharata

Lungwort

Zone 3

Boraginaceae (Forget-me-not family)

Also known as Bethlehem Sage

For a color illustration of *Pulmonaria officinalis,* see page 70.

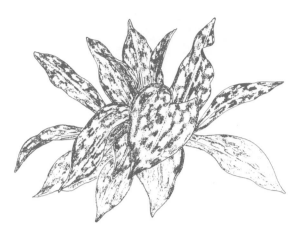

Lungwort is a deciduous, clump-forming, bristly plant that grows 1½ feet high. New foliage appears quite early in the spring. The leaves are mostly basal, and arise in thick whorls from the rhizomes. The flowers are borne in the spring on sparsely leafy stems above the foliage mass. This plant spreads by short rhizomes. Growth rate is medium. Texture is medium-coarse.

Leaves. The narrowly elliptic to elliptic leaves are simple, entire, and dark green generously spotted with white. The basal leaves are long-petioled; the few stem leaves are alternate.

Flowers. The flowers are produced in nodding, terminal cymes from April through May before the leaves are fully mature. They are pink to rose in bud, and blue to violet when fully open. Each flower has a 5-toothed, tubular calyx and a corolla with a narrow tube and 5 spreading lobes.

Culture. Lungwort grows best in partial to full shade in a cool, moist, well-drained, humus-rich soil. Hot or dry locations cause the leaves to become brown and crisp along the margins.

Lungwort should be watered during dry weather and thinned when the plants become overcrowded. This plant requires little other attention.

Plant in the early spring or very early fall. Incorporate peat moss, well-rotted compost, or other organic matter into the planting bed. Transplants (especially those planted in the fall) should be kept well watered until the root system has developed. Apply 2 to 3 inches of an organic mulch to conserve moisture and control weeds until the planting has covered the area.

To obtain uniform plants, propagate by division in late summer or early fall. Although Lungwort can also be grown from seeds, it hybridizes freely, and the seedlings are subject to wide variation.

This plant is not seriously affected by insect pests or diseases.

Uses. Lungwort can be used effectively as a ground cover beneath shrubs and deciduous trees and as an edging and border plant. It is valued for its attractive foliage and flowers.

Pulmonaria saccharata is native to Europe. The spotted leaves of the related *Pulmonaria officinalis* resemble a diseased lung, and this plant was once believed to have medicinal qualities that were helpful in treating lung disorders. *Pulmo* of the genus name is the Latin word for "lung."

The species of *Pulmonaria* are not easily distinguished because they hybridize readily, giving rise to wide variation, particularly in flower color. Many of these plants have been selected and given cultivar names that are listed commercially.

Pulmonaria saccharata 'Mrs. Moon' is a recommended selection. This plant has large, pink buds that open to showy, gentian blue flowers.

Pulmonaria angustifolia (Blue Cowslip, Lungwort) is a closely related species. It has bright, unspotted, green leaves. The pink-to-rose flower buds gradually mature to blue flowers. This plant is slightly smaller than *Pulmonaria saccharata* (usually growing less than 1 foot high), and its cultural requirements and uses are identical. 'Azurea' and 'April Opal' are intensely blue selections of *Pulmonaria angustifolia;* 'Rubra' is a nearly red or deep-reddish violet form; and 'Alba' is a white-flowered form. *Pulmonaria angustifolia* is native to Europe.

Another related species is *Pulmonaria officinalis* (Jerusalem Cowslip, Jerusalem Sage, Lungwort). This plant has spotted leaves, and the bases of the leaves are heart-shaped or lobed. It is usually less than 1 foot high. The flowers are rose-violet to blue and occasionally reddish. *Pulmonaria officinalis* is native to Europe.

Ranunculus repens

Creeping Buttercup

Zone 3

Ranunculaceae (Buttercup family)

Also known as Butter Daisy, Creeping Crowfoot, Sitfast, Yellow Gowan

For a color illustration of *Ranunculus repens,* see page 71.

Creeping Buttercup is a vigorous, somewhat hairy ground cover that spreads rapidly by runners that root at their nodes. These runners may grow up to 2 feet long or longer during the growing season. Most of the leaves are basal. They arise from the crowns or are borne along the runners, forming a foliage mass that is usually about ½ to 1 foot high. Creeping Buttercup is a deciduous plant, dying to the ground in late autumn. The flowers are produced above the foliage on slender stalks that rise 1 to 2 feet high. Texture is medium-fine.

Leaves. The dark-green, nearly round leaves are deeply divided into 3 lobes; each lobe is divided into 3 coarsely toothed lobules. The leaves are alternate and mostly long-stalked.

Flowers. The attractive, cup-shaped flowers are ½ to 1 inch wide, and are borne on erect, branched stalks. They are complete, consisting of 5 sepals, 5 glossy, bright-yellow petals, and many free stamens and pistils. Each petal is ¼ to ½ inch long, with a small nectary at the base. Creeping Buttercup has a relatively long flowering period, blooming from May to August.

Fruits. The fruits are small achenes with a persistent style. They are held in tight clusters.

Culture. Creeping Buttercup is easy to grow in almost any slightly acid to alkaline soil, and is well adapted to moist soils. It should be planted in areas of full sun to half shade. Although this plant may become weedy, it is easily controlled by cutting back the creeping runners before they root. Fertilize when the plants show symptoms of deficiencies. When grown in areas with high fertility, Creeping Buttercup may be

extremely difficult to control. To prevent rampant self-sowing, remove the faded flowers before the seed clusters mature.

Propagation is by seeds and division in the spring. Space plants 1 to 2 feet apart. Creeping Buttercup may be planted any time from early spring to early fall as long as it receives adequate moisture.

This plant is not seriously affected by insects or diseases. It is valued for its attractive flowers and easy maintenance.

Uses. Creeping Buttercup is best used in areas where its vigorous spread may be easily restricted, such as between a sidewalk and building. It is also suitable for naturalized locations, where it requires little attention and may spread unimpeded. Creeping Buttercup should not be combined with less vigorous plants.

Ranunculus repens is native to Eurasia, and has become naturalized throughout most of North America.

A recommended selection is the cultivar *Ranunculus repens* 'Pleniflorus', a showy, double-flowering form. This plant may also be listed as *Ranunculus repens* 'Flore Pleno' and *Ranunculus speciosus*.

Saponaria ocymoides

Rock Soapwort

Zone 3

Caryophyllaceae (Pink family)

For a color illustration of *Saponaria ocymoides*, see page 71.

Rock Soapwort forms broad, spreading mats of somewhat woody stems and semievergreen foliage. It grows 6 to 8 inches high, and spreads by underground shoots to 2 feet wide. The mounds are completely covered by masses of phloxlike flowers for a month or longer in late spring. Growth rate is medium to fast. Texture is medium-fine.

Leaves. The small, dark-green leaves are about 1 inch long, and are borne on reddish, freely branching stems. They are opposite, simple, and entire, and are usually elliptic (although they may be slightly broadened at the apex or base). The lower leaves are short-petioled; the upper leaves are sessile.

Flowers. Rock Soapwort flowers profusely for about 4 weeks from early June to mid-July, and then continues flowering sporadically until September. The bright, purplish pink flowers are 1/2 to 5/8 inch wide, and are borne in broad, loose cymes. Each flower has a tubular, 5-toothed calyx and 5 showy petals. The petals have a narrowed, petiolelike base; the upper 1/2 of the petal is expanded and flattened, and may be shallowly notched at the apex.

Culture. Rock Soapwort requires full sun. It grows well in almost any well-drained soil, especially sandy soil, but tolerates moderately poor soils. This plant will not tolerate slush, and areas where moisture accumulates in the winter are not suitable sites.

To prevent the plants from becoming unkempt, sprawling masses, cut them back severely after flowering. Apply a complete fertilizer 2 or 3 times during the growing season to maintain plant vigor. When snow cover is absent during severe winters, the planting may require a loose,

protective covering such as that given by evergreen branches.

This plant is easily grown from seed sown in the spring. It may also be propagated by division in very early spring and by cuttings taken in midsummer.

Rock Soapwort is somewhat difficult to transplant, and larger plants transplant poorly. Plant in spring or early fall. Space plants 2 feet apart, and keep them moist until they are well established.

This plant is not seriously affected by insect pests or diseases.

Uses. Rock Soapwort is often used in rock gardens, as an edging plant, and as a trailing plant over dry walls. It is an excellent ground cover on sunny slopes and in sandy soils, but it is not suitable for covering large areas or to control erosion. Rock Soapwort is valued for its relatively long period of bloom and its low, compact habit.

Saponaria ocymoides is native to the alpine regions of central and southern Europe. Certain species of *Saponaria* have detergent properties. When the leaves and roots are bruised, they expel juices that create a soapy lather when mixed with water. (The common name "Soapwort" refers to this characteristic. The Latin word for "soap" is *sapo.*)

A recommended selection is the cultivar *Saponaria ocymoides* 'Splendens', which has more intensely colored flowers and is often more readily available than the species. Two other cultivars, 'Rosea' (bright rose flowers) and 'Rubra' (deep red flowers), are also available to a limited extent.

138

Sedum species

Sedum

Crassulaceae (Stonecrop family)

Also known as Live-Forever, Stonecrop, Orpine

Sedum is the largest genus of the Stonecrop family, probably consisting of about 300 species. Most sedums are low, succulent, evergreen to deciduous perennials, although some are annuals and biennials. Many are mat-forming, with ground-hugging, vegetative shoots 1 to 2 or 3 inches high and ascending or erect flowering stems; others form tufts or clumps of ascending stems that may grow to nearly 18 inches high. Sedums may spread slowly to rapidly by their creeping stems, rooting at the nodes or by short rhizomes from a fairly static rootstock. In general, the matlike sedums are the most suitable for use as ground covers. Because the species combine well, however, mixed plantings of sedums with varying habits may also be used.

Leaves. Sedums are primarily grown for their attractive, colorful foliage. The leaves are usually hairless and smooth, and are often partially covered with a whitish wax. Color varies from bright green to blue- and gray-green, yellow-green, and reddish or purplish. The stalkless or short-petioled leaves are generally alternate or in spirals on the stems, and are often set so closely together that they overlap in a shinglelike pattern. The leaves are sometimes opposite or whorled, and may be flattened, cylindrical, egg-shaped, or almost spherical. The flattened leaves range from narrow and needlelike to nearly rounded, with margins that are entire or bluntly toothed. The leaves of vegetative stems and flowering shoots may also be dissimilar.

Flowers. The small, starlike flowers are produced for 2 to 4 weeks from early May to October. They are usually borne in 1-sided,

coiled cymes or in axillary or terminal corymbs that vary in habit from open to compact. The typical flower is symmetrical and complete, with fleshy sepals, spreading, elliptical petals, twice as many stamens as petals, and separate pistils that develop into small, podlike fruits. The sepals and petals (usually 5) may be free or slightly united basally. The flowers may be white, yellow, greenish, pink, reddish, or purple.

Culture. Sedums require a well-drained soil for winter survival. Many species grow best and develop a more compact habit in full sun; others thrive in light to heavy shade. Although the shade-tolerant sedums benefit from organic matter in the soil, most species thrive in soils with average to poor fertility and in sandy to rocky areas. Sedums are usually tolerant of heat and drouth, and will survive considerable neglect once they are established.

Some species spread vigorously and may become weedy. Because of their shallow root systems, these species are easy to eradicate. Cut the plants back to stimulate new growth or whenever they grow out of bounds.

Sedums are easily propagated by division at almost any time during the growing season. They may also be grown from stem and leaf cuttings taken in midsummer. For numerous species of sedums, any piece cut from a plant will root in moist soil. Plant in the spring or late summer. Space plants 9 to 18 inches apart.

Sedums are virtually pest free. Too much moisture may cause root and stem rots, and excessive water and nutrients may cause plants to grow out of character.

Uses. Sedums are widely used in rock gardens, in crevices of retaining walls, between paving stones, and as container plants. Those species that are suitable for use as ground-cover plants are generally good choices for hot, dry locations in full sun, especially in areas of thin soil over rock. The vigorous, weedy species are best used in areas where their growth may be restricted or in naturalized sites where they are allowed to spread. Sedums are long-lived plants that are valued for their attractive, often colorful foliage, interesting textural effects, vigor, and easy maintenance.

Sedum species are native throughout most of the temperate zones of the Northern Hemisphere, extending into the Southern Hemisphere only in Bolivia, Peru, East Africa, and Madagascar. The genus name is derived from the Latin word *sedo* (to sit or hold fast), a reference to the manner in which many species attach themselves to rock walls and outcroppings.

Although this genus has been studied extensively, the nomenclature is still quite confused. The degree of exposure to sunlight, soil type, and other environmental conditions can alter a plant's appearance (especially its leaf and flower color and compactness), making classification difficult.

Sedum acre

Goldmoss Sedum

Zone 3

Also known as Gold-Dust, Golden Carpet, Golden Moss, Love-Entangle, Mossy Stonecrop, Wallpepper

For a color illustration of *Sedum acre* 'Minus', see page 71.

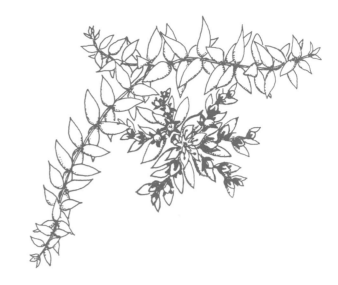

Goldmoss Sedum is a somewhat weedy evergreen species that has escaped cultivation and become naturalized in southern Canada and the northern United States. It forms broad, low mats of short, branching, prostrate stems about 2 inches high that root at their nodes as they creep. The plant is smooth and hairless, with yellow-green, succulent, triangular leaves that are almost as thick as they are broad. The tiny (less than ¼ inch long), stalkless leaves are arranged spirally on the stems, and are closely set and overlapping. Their margins are entire, and the apex is blunt pointed. Texture is fine.

The bright-yellow flowers are produced abundantly from early June to early July in terminal cymes on short, erect, leafy shoots that may grow 2 to 3 inches high. The flowers are ½ inch wide, with 5 fleshy, green sepals, 5 lance-shaped petals, 10 stamens, and 5 pistils.

Goldmoss Sedum thrives in full sun in almost any soil, including alkaline and very thin, poor, dry soils. This plant should be grown in areas where little else will grow, and where it may easily be contained or allowed to spread freely. It seeds itself readily. Because nearly any small segment will root wherever it falls, Goldmoss Sedum may become invasive. In the Midwest, it is not as vigorous when grown in the shade.

A smaller, more compact form is the cushion-like cultivar 'Minus'. This plant, which may also be sold as *Sedum acre* 'Minimum', grows well in both sun and shade, and is one of the best sedums for use as a ground cover.

Sedum album

White Stonecrop

Zone 4

Also known as Worm-Grass

White Stonecrop is a smooth, hairless, mat-forming ground cover that grows 3 to 6 inches high and spreads rapidly by creeping, prostrate stems that root along their lengths. Its alternate, stalkless, evergreen leaves are ⅛ to ⅝ inch long, and are cylindrical or somewhat flattened, with a rounded apex. They become slightly red tinged in winter.

The white flowers are borne in loose, terminal panicles from mid-July to late August. They are held on leafy shoots about 2 inches above the mass of stems and foliage. Each flower has a short pedicel, 5 sepals, 5 narrow, elliptical petals, 10 stamens, and 5 erect pistils.

White Stonecrop grows best in poor soil in open, arid locations of full sun to semishade. It may be somewhat invasive. Space plants 12 to 18 inches apart.

The cultivars Sedum album 'Murale' (may be listed as Sedum murale) and 'Purpureum' have purplish leaves and pale-pink flowers. 'Chloroticum' has vivid yellow-green leaves and greenish white flowers.

Sedum kamtschaticum

Kamchatka Sedum

Zone 3

Also known as Orange Stonecrop

Kamchatka Sedum forms small, cushionlike mounds 3 to 4 inches high. Its weakly ascending, nonrooting stems may grow up to 12 inches in length, trailing along the ground and turning upward at their apices. This plant spreads slowly by short rhizomes. Texture is medium-fine.

The glossy, dark-green leaves are ½ to 2 inches long, and are borne alternately. They are flat, rather thin, and spoon-shaped to lance-shaped, with the toothed, broader end towards the apex. The foliage turns bronze to gold in the autumn.

The bright-orangish yellow flowers are produced in flat clusters of 25 or fewer from early July to mid-September. The flowers are about ¾ inch wide, with 5 sepals, 5 petals, 10 stamens, and 5 pistils. Kamchatka Sedum requires full sun and tolerates very poor soils. Space plants 9 to 12 inches apart.

The subspecies Ellacombianum (may be listed as Sedum ellacombianum) is also an attractive plant with scalloped, light-green leaves and flowers about ½ inch wide. Another subspecies, Middendorffianum, has narrow, dark-green leaves and rounded teeth only toward the apex, and resembles Iberis sempervirens (Candytuft) when it is not in flower. Its flowers are slightly over ½ inch wide. The species and subspecies are excellent ground-cover plants, and should be used more widely in the landscape.

Sedum reflexum

Jenny Stonecrop

Zone 3

Also known as Creeping Jenny, Yellow
Stonecrop

Jenny Stonecrop is a smooth, hairless, carpeting
plant with branching, prostrate stems that form
loose mats. Its alternate, evergreen leaves are
closely set on the stems. They are narrowly
cylindrical (¼ to ½ inch long and ¹⁄₁₆ to ⅛ inch
wide), with a pointed apex.

The golden yellow flowers are borne terminally
from late June to August in rounded cymes on
ascending stems 6 to 13 inches long. The clusters
are nodding in the bud stage, becoming erect as
the flowers mature. The parts of the ½-inch-wide
flowers are in whorls of 5 to 7, with twice as
many stamens as petals. The plants are 8 to 10
inches high when in flower.

Jenny Stonecrop is sometimes confused with
Sedum rupestre. The latter is not cold-hardy, and
is used as a ground-cover plant in mild climates.

Sedum sarmentosum

Stringy Stonecrop

Zone 3

Stringy Stonecrop is a rampantly growing,
prostrate sedum that forms mats up to 6 inches
high. The evergreen leaves are ½ to 1 inch long
and ¼ inch wide, and are borne in whorls of 3 on
long, creeping, branching stems that root at their
nodes. The flattish, succulent, pale-green to
yellow-green leaves are elliptical to broadly
lance-shaped; they narrow slightly at their base,
forming a short petiole.

The sulphur yellow flowers are produced in
June on ascending, flowering stems in loose,
3-forked cymes. The 5-parted, stalkless flowers
are ⅝ inch wide, and are subtended by bracts
that are similar to but smaller than the vegetative
stem leaves.

Stringy Stonecrop escaped from cultivation,
and has become widely naturalized in northeastern North America. Although this plant does
not produce viable seed, any small segment will
root and grow when it is in contact with moist
soil. Stringy Stonecrop should be grown where
it can easily be restrained, and in arid, rocky
areas where little else will grow. It flourishes
in full sun and poor soils.

Sedum sexangulare

Hexagon Stonecrop

Zone 2

Sedum spathulifolium

Zone 4

Hexagon Stonecrop is an evergreen plant with creeping stems that form broad mats 3 to 4 inches high. The linear, almost cylindrical leaves are spirally arranged and crowded on the stems, appearing 6-ranked; they are ⅛ to ¼ inch long, with a blunt apex.

The canary yellow flowers are ⅜ inch wide, and are borne terminally during June and July atop ascending stems 3 to 6 inches long. They are clustered in flat, 3-branched cymes.

Hexagon Stonecrop is similar to *Sedum acre* (see page 141), differing slightly in leaf shape and flower size. It is also more restrained in habit and spreads moderately.

Sedum spathulifolium produces rosettes of evergreen foliage that form dense mats 2 to 4 inches high. The rosettes give rise to offsets, and send out horizontal stems that terminate in a rooting rosette that also produces offsets. The rate of spread is slow. Texture is fine.

The flat, fleshy leaves are ½ to 1¼ inches long and spoon-shaped, with a blunt apex. They are usually covered with a mealy, whitish wax that makes them appear bluish green, although they are also sometimes red tinged. The flowers are borne during May and June atop ascending, leafy shoots that may grow 6 inches long. The leaves of these flowering shoots are alternate, narrowly oblong, and lack a petiole. The sessile or short-stalked, bright-yellow flowers are usually clustered into 3-branched cymes. They are slightly more than ½ inch wide, with 5 sepals and 5 widely spreading petals.

Sedum spathulifolium grows best in sun in a well-drained soil. Although this plant is tolerant of light shade, it is more compact and develops better foliage color in full sun. Space plants 9 inches apart.

Sedum spathulifolium is not as widely cultivated as some of its superior cultivars. Among these are 'Capa Blanca', with attractive, faintly fragrant, silvery foliage (created by a thick, waxy leaf coating), and 'Purpureum', with purplish to bluish purple-tinged leaves.

Sedum spectabile

Showy Stonecrop

Zone 3

Also known as Ice Plant

Showy Stonecrop is a clump-forming sedum with thick, erect, unbranched stems that arise from a fairly static rootstock. Its neat, dense mounds of foliage (12 to 18 inches high), are attractive throughout the growing season, and are topped in late summer by large, pink flower clusters. The stems die to the ground with the first hard frost.

The stems and fleshy, flat leaves are smooth and hairless. They are pale grayish green and cool to the touch, giving rise to the common name Ice Plant. The leaves are opposite, in whorls of 3 or 4, or alternate. They are egg-shaped (about 3 inches long and 2 inches wide), with a sparsely serrate margin.

The pink flowers are ½ inch wide, and are borne terminally from late August to mid-September in flat clusters 3 to 4 inches wide that cover the top of the plant. They have 5 sepals, 5 slightly concave petals, 10 stamens that are longer than the petals, and 5 pistils. Butterflies find these flowers particularly attractive.

Showy Stonecrop is one of the showiest, most durable, and commonly cultivated sedums that is grown in the perennial border and rock garden. It thrives in full sun to light shade in almost any soil, including moist, well-drained soils and soils of average to poor fertility. Very fertile soils may cause weak, leggy growth, with the clumps falling apart. When massed, Showy Stonecrop is an excellent ground cover for an open location. For an interesting effect, the masses may be alternated with rock-mulched areas. Showy Stonecrop also combines well with other sedums and gray and silver foliage plants for a mixed ground-cover planting. Plant in the spring. Space plants 18 inches apart.

Many selections of Showy Stonecrop are available commercially, including 'Album', a white-flowering form, and 'Star Dust', which has ivory-white flowers. 'Brilliant', 'Carmen', and 'Meteor' have deep rosy pink flowers. 'Variegatum' has foliage variegated with white and yellow, although the stems may revert to the all-green form.

Sedum spurium

Two-row Stonecrop

Zone 3

Also known as Creeping Sedum

For a color illustration of *Sedum spurium* 'Dragon's Blood', see page 71.

Two-row Stonecrop is a smooth, hairless, carpeting plant with freely branching stems that creep along the ground and root at their nodes, forming a mat 2 to 4 inches high. The stems are prostrate with ascending tips. The leaves are deciduous, except for the closely set clusters at the apices of the stems that turn reddish and persist throughout the winter. The rate of spread is moderate to rapid. Texture is medium-fine.

The opposite, dark-green, flat leaves are ½ to 1¼ inches long and about ⅔ as wide. They have a wedge-shaped base that narrows into a short petiole and a rounded apex. The leaf margin is serrate, with rounded teeth only towards the apex.

Two-row Stonecrop flowers from mid-July to early August. The flowers, which are usually pink but may vary from almost white to purplish, are borne in dense (usually 4-branched) cymes about 2 inches above the foliage atop reddish, ascending, flowering stems. They are ½ to ¾ inch wide, with 5 sepals, 5 petals that are twice the size of the sepals, 10 stamens with reddish anthers, and 5 pistils.

Two-row Stonecrop requires a well-drained soil, and grows best in a sunny location. Although it is tolerant of shade, foliage color will not be as vivid and thinning may occur. This plant is most suitable for rocky, exposed slopes and other arid sites. It may be somewhat weedy. Two-row Stonecrop is sometimes confused with *Sedum stoloniferum*.

Many selections of *Sedum spurium* are listed commercially; some of these are difficult to distinguish from one another. 'Album' is a white-flowering form. 'Coccineum' and 'Splendens' are names generally applied to deep red-pink flowering forms. 'Dragon's Blood' or 'Schorbusser Blut', a widely promoted ground cover, has new foliage that is bronze tinged, becoming red as autumn approaches. Its flowers are scarlet red. Although 'Dragon's Blood' is an excellent plant, it is not (advertisements to the contrary) the most suitable ground cover for every landscape. There is confusion among these selections. Plants listed as *Sedum coccineum*, *Sedum spurium* 'Coccineum', and *Sedum spurium* 'Splendens' may also be called Dragon's Blood Sedum.

Sempervivum species

Houseleek

Crassulaceae (Stonecrop family)

Also known as Live-Forever, Hen-and-Chickens, Old-Man-and-Woman

For a color illustration of *Sempervivum* species, see page 71.

The houseleeks comprise a genus of about 40 species of durable, long-lived succulents. Their fleshy, evergreen leaves grow in tight, flat rosettes that may be 6 inches wide when mature. These plants spread by short stolons, forming new plants (offsets) around their bases and creating dense mats of rosettes of various sizes. The starlike flowers are borne in clusters atop stout, erect, leafy stems that grow from 2 to 18 inches high (depending upon the species) and arise from the center of a mature rosette. After flowering, the rosette dies and is replaced by the offsets that it produced. Most *Sempervivum* species flower in midsummer and spread rapidly.

Leaves. The thick, stalkless leaves are alternate, oblong to broadly egg-shaped, and attached at their broad bases. They range in texture from smooth to varying degrees of hairiness and in color from every shade of green to bronze to bluish or gray (caused by a whitish, waxy coating on the leaves). Some houseleeks have leaves that are tipped or margined with pink, red, purple, or brown. Leaf color may be altered somewhat by the plant's exposure to sunlight and other environmental conditions. Depending upon the species, the leaves may be held in either loose or in compact rosettes.

Flowers. The very small, bisexual flowers are usually borne terminally on stout, leafy stalks in 1-sided, compact cymes, and may have from 6 to 20 narrow, lance-shaped, distinct (free) sepals and the same number of petals. The petals vary in color from greenish to yellow, red, purple, and white, and their margins may be fringed or lined with hairs (ciliate).

Each flower has twice as many stamens as petals.

Culture. Houseleeks grow best in a well-drained soil in full sun to partial shade. Good drainage is essential. In alpine regions, where many houseleeks are native, they grow in rock cracks and crevices, and are tolerant of the thinnest soils and driest conditions.

These plants are tolerant of most poor soils if they are well drained. Houseleeks do not require regular fertilization. They should not be grown in combination with very aggressive plants because they do not tolerate competition well. The planting should be weeded, and dead rosettes should be removed so that surrounding rosettes can fill in more quickly.

Houseleeks are most easily propagated by separating rooted offsets, although they may also be grown from seeds. Since these plants do not flower until they are mature, seeds may not be produced every year. The seedlings are also subject to wide variation.

Houseleeks are susceptible to crown rot and rust in damp locations or during prolonged periods of wet weather. When they are grown in dry areas with good drainage, however, they are problem-free and very tenacious.

147

Uses. Houseleeks are traditional rock-garden and dry-wall plants. They can also be used effectively as ground covers in dry, sun-baked locations, especially in combination with some of the less aggressive sedums (see pages 142-145) that grow in a similar environment. Combinations of houseleeks with various foliage colors and rosettes are quite attractive. Houseleeks may also be grown as house plants if they are left outdoors until after Chistmas so that their rest period is satisfied; they will then bloom and reproduce. These plants are valued for their rugged durability, unusual, crisp texture, and ease of cultivation.

Most *Sempervivum* species are native to the mountainous regions of central and southern Europe. *Sempervivum* is from the Latin *semper vivo*, "to live forever." In the middle ages, these plants were grown on house roofs in Europe because it was thought that they would ward off lightning and other potential disasters.

Only a few species and their numerous variants and hybrids are offered commercially. The nomenclature of the houseleeks is quite confused, and many of these plants are incorrectly named. Nurseries that specialize in alpine and rock-garden plants are most likely to offer the greatest variety of houseleeks.

Sempervivum arachnoideum

Cobweb Houseleek
Zone 5

Also known as Spiderweb Houseleek

For a color illustration of *Sempervivum arachnoideum* var. *tomentosum*, see page 72.

Cobweb Houseleek, one of the most unusual and ornamental species of *Sempervivum*, forms rosettes of about 50 leaves that may grow to 1½ inches wide. The green-and-red leaves are abruptly short-pointed at their apices, and are connected by silvery strands of cobweblike hairs. The bright-red flowers, which are produced in July, are more attractive than those of most houseleeks. They are ½ to 1 inch wide, and are borne in clusters on stalks 3 to 5 inches long. This plant requires a drier environment than any other species of houseleek. In damp, humid areas, its hairs hold moisture, causing the rosettes to rot.

Sempervivum arachnoideum var. *tomentosum* is more densely covered with long, silvery hairs than the species.

Sempervivum tectorum

Common Houseleek
Zone 4

Common Houseleek forms somewhat open, flat rosettes that usually grow 3 to 4 inches wide, with 50 to 60 smooth, hairless, green or purple-tipped leaves per rosette. The leaves may grow to 3 inches long. The purplish red flowers are ¾ to 1 inch wide, and are borne in July and August atop a densely hairy stem 8 to 18 inches high. They have up to 13 sepals and the same number of petals. This vigorous species and its many variants are the most widely cultivated of the houseleeks. They are often listed under obsolete or incorrect botanical names.

Sempervivum tectorum 'Robustum' has purple-tipped leaves that form rosettes up to 6 inches wide.

Sempervivum tectorum var. *alpinum* (may be listed as *Sempervivum alpinum*) has smaller rosettes (1 to 2½ inches wide) and red leaf bases.

Sempervivum tectorum var. *calcareum* (may be listed as *Sempervivum calcareum*) has pale-red flowers and leaves that are covered with a whitish wax and have distinct brown-purple tips.

Verbena canadensis

Rose Verbena

Zone 5

Verbenaceae (Vervain family)

Also known as Clump Verbena, Creeping Vervain, Midland Vervain, Rose Vervain

For a color illustration of *Verbena canadensis*, see page 72.

Rose Verbena is a deciduous, highly branched ground cover that forms mounds ½ to 1½ feet high. The somewhat trailing stems may grow to 3 feet long; they root at nodes that contact moist soil. The magenta flowers almost conceal the foliage in late spring. Growth rate is rapid. Texture is medium-coarse.

Leaves. The opposite, dark-green leaves are usually produced on square stems. The leaves and stems may be covered with short, stiff hairs or almost hairless. The leaves are 2 to 4 inches long, egg-shaped to oblong, and sharply and irregularly toothed. They may be weakly to decidedly 3-cleft or lobed.

Flowers. The bisexual flowers are produced in great abundance from late May through June, and then sporadically until the first heavy frost in early autumn. The color and color intensity vary from reddish purple and lilac to rose. The flowers are borne in short, dense, terminal spikes; these spikes elongate as the flowers mature and the fruits are formed. Each flower is subtended by bristle bracts that are shorter than the calyx. The tubular calyx is sharply 5-toothed and encircles the tube of the corolla. The corolla flares into 5 spreading, unequal lobes above the calyx. There are 4 paired stamens.

Culture. Rose Verbena grows best in partial shade in a moderately fertile, slightly acid to neutral soil. It is somewhat drouth-tolerant (frequently growing in sandy soil in its native habitats), and is fairly tolerant of infertile soils. This plant is very easy to grow.

Remove the faded flower heads for prolonged heavy flowering. Without adequate snow cover, Rose Verbena may be winter-killed, and a protective mulch of evergreen branches may be necessary during severe winters. Otherwise, this plant requires little care. In locations where it is particularly well suited, however, it may become rampant and weedy.

The easiest methods of propagation are by division in the spring and by stem cuttings taken in July. Rose Verbena is also readily grown from seeds, although seedlings will not flower until the second year. Plant in the spring. Space plants 1 to 2 feet apart.

Uses. Rose Verbena is an excellent ground cover for sunny banks and slopes. It is valued for its very long flowering period.

Verbena canadensis is native from Virginia to Florida, and westward to Colorado and Mexico.

Recommended selections include *Verbena canadensis* 'Candidissima', which has white flowers, and 'Compacta', which is lower growing and more dense than the species. 'Rosea' is also more compact than the species, and flowers more prolifically over a longer period.

150

Veronica species

Speedwell

Scrophulariaceae (Foxglove family)

Veronica is a very large genus composed of approximately 300 species of annual and perennial plants that vary widely in habit. Some of these plants form clumps of erect stems that spread by slowly creeping rootstocks; others have trailing stems that mound upon themselves or form very low mats of prostrate stems that often root at the nodes. Many of these are excellent, long-lived border, rock garden, and ground-cover plants; a few species are well known as rampant lawn weeds. Texture is fine to medium.

Leaves. The simple leaves are deciduous to semievergreen in northern regions, and are often evergreen in mild climates. The stems may be branched or unbranched. The lower stem leaves are usually opposite, and the upper leaves are alternate. The leaves may be broadly oval or egg-shaped to very narrowly lance-shaped, with entire or toothed margins.

Flowers. Speedwells bloom from May through August. The small, perfect flowers are usually produced in clusters in terminal or (occasionally) axillary spikes or racemes, but may also be solitary. They vary from nearly to completely regular, with a 4-toothed calyx, 4-lobed corolla, 2 stamens, and a single pistil. The typical speedwell corolla has a short tube and open, spreading lobes (3 lobes are often rounded; the lower, fourth lob is smaller and narrower). The corolla is usually blue to purplish, but may be pink or white.

Culture. Speedwells are easy to grow in almost any moderately acid to alkaline soil that is moist and well drained (good drainage is essential to their winter survival). A soil of only average fertility is preferable; species may spread rampantly or grow tall and leggy in rich soils. They thrive in areas of full sun to light shade; a few species are tolerant of half-shade or more.

Many of the low-growing speedwells are shallow-rooted, requiring regular watering whenever rainfall is inadequate. Incorporate 2 to 3 inches of peat moss or well-rotted organic matter into the planting bed to aid in moisture retention. Fertilize in early spring with a complete fertilizer. It is important to water fertilizers in immediately because the foliage of speedwells is easily burned.

Plantings may be cut back after flowering to remove the withered flower clusters and promote new growth. Flowering of some of the taller, clump-forming species is prolonged by removing the faded flowers.

Propagation is by division of rootstocks or by separation of the rooted stems in early spring or after flowering in late summer. Many of the taller, clump-forming speedwells need to be divided and reset every 4 to 5 years in order to rejuvenate growth.

Speedwells are essentially insect and disease free. Leaf spots and downy mildew may be problems in very warm, humid weather.

Uses. Speedwells are common plants in the flower border. The low-growing and matlike speedwells are also often used in rock gardens, as edging plants, and as fillers in stone walks and terraces. Many of these species are also excellent ground-cover plants for locations in full sun and beneath high, open shade trees. Speedwells are valued for their attractive summer flowers and easy maintenance.

Vernonica species are widely distributed, and are mostly native to temperate regions of the Northern Hemisphere. The genus name commemorates Saint Veronica

Veronica chamaedrys

Germander Speedwell

Zone 3

Also known as Angel's-eye, Bird's-eye

Germander Speedwell is a compact, rather hairy ground-cover plant that spreads rapidly by short stolons, forming clumps up to 1½ feet high. In some regions, it has escaped cultivation and become a weed. The semievergreen leaves are ½ to 1½ inches long, and are arranged oppositely on ascending stems. The leaves are sessile (lack a petiole), and are broadly egg-shaped, with a distinctly toothed margin and heart-shaped base.

The flowers are a vivid blue with a light eye, and are produced during May and June in loose racemes 4 to 6 inches long. Germander Speedwell grows best in full sun or light shade. It should be used in areas where it can be easily restricted, or in naturalized plantings where it can be allowed to spread.

The cultivar *Veronica chamaedrys* 'Alba' is a white-flowering form.

Veronica incana

Woolly Speedwell

Zone 3

For a color illustration of *Veronica incana*, see page 72.

Woolly Speedwell is a densely hairy ground-cover plant. Its stems and leaves are covered with whitish hairs that make the plant appear a soft, silvery gray. The semievergreen, mostly basal foliage forms a loose mat that is less than 1 foot high when not in flower. The stalked, oblong to lance-shaped leaves are up to 3 inches long, with margins toothed with rounded teeth. Growth rate is medium. Texture is medium.

The foliage of Woolly Speedwell is quite attractive, and its bright lilac-blue flowers contrast strikingly with the silvery leaves. The flowers are held above the foliage in slender, terminal racemes 4 to 6 inches long, making the plant 12 inches or more high when in flower. Woolly Speedwell blooms from mid-June to late July.

This plant must be grown in full sun. The soil must be perfectly drained to insure winter survival.

The cultivar *Veronica incana* 'Rosea' has rose-pink flowers that combine with the silver foliage to create a soft effect.

Veronica officinalis

Common Speedwell

Zone 5

Also known as Drug Speedwell, Gypsyweed

Common Speedwell is a hairy ground-cover plant that forms mats 6 to 12 inches high of prostrate and somewhat ascending stems that root wherever they touch moist soil. The evergreen, oval to oblong leaves are up to 2 inches long, with a serrate margin.

The pale-blue, ½-inch-wide flowers are produced from mid-May to mid-July in erect, dense, usually axillary racemes. This plant requires little care. It thrives in full sun to dense shade, and is somewhat drouth-tolerant. Common Speedwell is probably the best *Veronica* species for use as a ground cover. It is vigorous and spreads rapidly.

Veronica prostrata

Rock Speedwell

Zone 4

Also known as Harebell Speedwell

May be listed as *Veronica rupestris, Veronica latifolia* var. *prostrata*

Rock Speedwell is a nearly evergreen ground-cover plant that forms dense, widespreading mats of prostrate stems. The flowers are borne terminally on erect stems, making the plant up to 10 inches high when in flower. Texture is medium-fine.

The dark-green leaves are about 1½ inches long, and narrowly egg-shaped to linear, with an entire or sparsely toothed margin. The deep-blue flowers are produced in racemes during May and June. Rock Speedwell grows best in a well-drained, fertile soil in sun to light shade. It is somewhat more drouth-resistant than most other *Veronica* species. This plant is a good choice for use between paving stones of walks and terraces.

Veronica prostrata 'Heavenly Blue' is a selection with sapphire blue flowers.

Veronica repens

Creeping Speedwell

Zone 5

For a color illustration of *Veronica repens*, see page 72.

Creeping Speedwell is a semievergreen to deciduous ground-cover plant that forms relatively uniform mats 4 to 6 inches high. It spreads rapidly by creeping stems that root wherever they touch moist soil. Texture is fine.

The small, glossy, dark-green leaves are smooth, with a margin that is slightly toothed with blunt teeth. The narrowly egg-shaped leaves are ½ inch long.

Creeping Speedwell flowers during May and June. The bluish flowers are ¼ inch wide, and are borne profusely in few-flowered racemes that almost obscure the foliage.

This plant grows best in a moist, well-drained, acidic soil in full sun to half shade.

Waldsteinia ternata

Barren Strawberry

Zone 4

Rosaceae (Rose family)

Also known as Dry Strawberry, Yellow Strawberry

For a color illustration of *Waldsteinia ternata*, see page 72.

Barren Strawberry is an evergreen ground cover that forms compact mats of strawberrylike foliage 4 to 6 inches high and spreads by short, shallow rhizomes. The plants are covered in the spring by a profusion of showy, yellow flowers that rise 3 to 4 inches above the foliage. Unlike true strawberries, Barren Strawberry does not produce showy or edible fruits. Growth rate is medium. Texture is medium.

Leaves. The glossy, bright-green leaves are mostly basal, and are divided into 3 short-stalked leaflets ½ to 1¼ inches long. The leaflets, wedge-shaped, with a more or less rounded apex, are irregularly toothed and lobed on the upper margin. The older leaves turn a wine red in winter.

Flowers. The bright-yellow flowers are borne from early May through June. They are produced singly or in 2- to 7-flowered corymbs on bracted stalks that rise to about the same height as the foliage. Each flower is complete, and is composed of numerous stamens, 5 showy, yellow petals, and 5 leafy sepals that alternate with 5 small, often deciduous bractlets. They are about ¾ inch wide when fully open.

Fruits. The fruits are small, brown achenes.

Culture. Barren Strawberry grows well in almost any moist, well-drained acid to neutral soil (pH range from 4 to 7). It thrives in full sun to partial shade, and tolerates periods of drouth if well shaded.

Plant Barren Strawberry in a well-prepared bed. Incorporate 1 to 2 inches of decayed organic matter or peat moss to aid moisture retention. A fine-textured mulch (such as pine needles) or well-rotted compost should be used until the planting bed has completely filled in. This plant requires little care, but it must be watered during dry weather if it is not shaded. For best growth, apply a complete fertilizer each spring and water immediately to prevent burning of the foliage.

Plant Barren Strawberry in the spring. Space plants 1 foot apart. The easiest method of propagation is by division, although Barren Strawberry may also be grown from seeds. This plant is not seriously affected by insects or diseases.

Uses. Barren Strawberry is particularly effective as a filler among large shrubs and small ornamental trees that provide partial shade. This plant is valued for its glossy, evergreen foliage, yellow flowers, and easy maintenance.

Waldsteinia ternata is native from central Europe to Siberia and Japan.

Waldsteinia fragarioides (also named Barren Strawberry) is a closely related species. Slightly larger and not as glossy as *Waldsteinia ternata*, this plant grows 8 to 10 inches high, and has leaflets that are 1 to 2 inches long. The flowers are borne in corymbs of 3 to 8 flowers. The cultural requirements and uses are the same as those for *Waldsteinia ternata*. *Waldsteinia fragarioides* is sometimes confused with and sold as *Waldsteinia ternata*. *Waldsteinia fragarioides* is native to wooded areas from New Brunswick to Minnesota, and south to Georgia and Missouri.

Another related species is *Waldsteinia geoides* (Russian Barren Strawberry). This plant is larger and less compact than *Waldsteinia ternata*, growing 12 inches or more high. The dull, rough leaves are 3 to 10 inches long. Russian Barren Strawberry is inferior to *Waldsteinia ternata* as a ground-cover plant because the long petioles bend over, exposing the soil at the center of the plant. *Waldsteinia geoides* is native to Hungary and the Balkans.

Glossary

Index
Botanical names
Common names

References

Glossary

Achene. A small, dry, 1-seeded fruit that remains closed at maturity.

Alternate. Leaves arranged singly at different heights and on different sides of the stem.

Anther. The pollen-bearing part of a stamen; usually borne at the top of the filament. See illustration, page 163.

Apetalous. A flower composed without petals.

Auriculate. Having auricles; an earlobe-shaped appendage, usually at the base of a leaf, petal, or bract.

Awl-shaped. Tapering gradually to a stiff, fine point, as an awl-shaped leaf.

Axil. Angular space between a leaf and the stem. See illustration of a petiole, page 161.

Axillary. Situated in an axil.

Bipinnate. A pinnate leaf with leaflets that are also pinnately divided. See **Pinnate.**

Bisexual. Flowers with both male (stamen) and female (pistil) reproductive parts.

Biternate. A ternate leaf with leaflets that are also ternately divided. See **Ternate.**

Bloom. See **Glaucous.**

Bract. A modified leaf borne on a floral axis or subtending a flower. See illustration, page 163.

Calyx. The outer set of floral parts that are commonly leafy but may be petallike. See illustration, page 163.

Campanulate. Bell-shaped.

Capsule. A dry, usually many-seeded fruit that arises from a compound pistil and splits open along 2 or more sutures. See **Dehiscent.**

Catkin. A spikelike, usually pendulous inflorescence that resembles a cat's tail in shape, as in the birch tree or willow.

Chlorosis. A yellowing caused by the failure of chlorophyll to develop in the plant tissues. This condition can result from a nutrient deficiency, virus, bacterium, or fungus.

Ciliate. Having margins, as of a leaf, that are fringed with hairs.

achene

auriculate

alternate leaves

awl-shaped leaf

bipinnate leaf

biternate leaf

campanulate flower

capsule

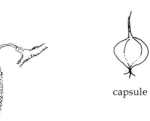
catkin

Compound leaf. A leaf composed of 2 or more leaflets on a common petiole.

Complete fertilizer. A fertilizer that contains the major plant nutrients: nitrogen (N), phosphorus (P), and potassium (K).

Cordate. Heart-shaped, with the point at the apex.

Corolla. The petals of a flower. See illustration, page 163.

Corymb. A more or less flat-topped, indeterminate inflorescence in which the outer flowers open first. See illustration, page 163.

Cyme. A determinate inflorescence, usually broad and more or less flat-topped, in which the central or terminal flower opens first. See illustration, page 163.

Decumbent stems. Stems that spread along the ground with ascending tips.

Dehiscent. Splitting open by pores or slits, as anthers and seed pods. See illustration of a pod, page 161.

Determinate. A type of inflorescence in which the terminal flower opens first, causing the flowering stem to stop growing. See **Indeterminate.**

Diploid. The basic number of chromosomes (2 sets) in most living cells. See **Triploid** and **Tetraploid.**

Disk flower. One of the symmetrical, tubular flowers on the head of a plant belonging to Asteraceae (Sunflower family). See **Ray flower.**

Drupe. A fleshy, 1-seeded fruit, such as a cherry or plum; a stone fruit.

Entire leaf. A leaf whose margin does not have teeth or indentations.

Exserted. Projecting beyond.

Filament. The stalk that bears the anther in a stamen. See illustration, page 163.

Follicle. A dry, many-seeded fruit that arises from a simple pistil and splits open along only 1 suture.

Glabrous. Without hairs; smooth.

Glaucous. Covered with a "bloom" (a white or pale-blue, powdery or waxy coating that rubs off easily, as in the grape or plum).

Impressed. As if marked by pressure, furrowed.

Indeterminate. A type of inflorescence in which the terminal flower opens last so that growth of the flowering stem is not stopped by the first flower. See **Determinate.**

Inflorescence. The arrangement of flowers on a stem; the flowering part of a plant. See illustrations, page 163.

Keeled. A longitudinal ridge on a leaf resembling the keel of a boat.

Lenticel. A small, corky pore on young bark through which gases are exchanged.

Nectary. A nectar-secreting gland.

Node. A joint or point on a stem at which a leaf or leaves are attached.

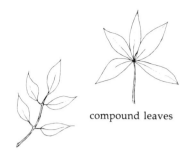

compound leaves

cordate

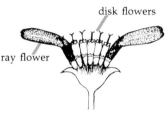

disk flowers

ray flower

disk flower

drupe

entire leaf

follicle

Ochrea (Ocrea). A tubular sheath formed by the fusion of 2 stipules at the stem nodes. Characteristic of Polygonaceae (Smartweed family).

Odd-pinnate. See **Pinnate.**

Offset. A short, horizontal branch that grows from a crown and bears buds and leafy rosettes.

Opposite. Leaves arranged in pairs at different heights on a stem, each separated from the other by ½ the circumference of the stem.

Ovary. The rounded, usually basal part of the pistil that bears the ovules. See illustration, page 163.

Ovule. The egg-containing unit of the ovary that becomes the seed after fertilization.

Palmate. Having parts arising from a common point, as fingers of a hand. May refer to venation, lobing, or compounding of a leaf.

Panicle. An indeterminate inflorescence, with repeated branching of spikes, racemes, corymbs, or umbels. See illustration, page 163.

Pedicel (Pedicle). The stalk of an individual flower.

Peduncle. The primary stalk of a flower or flower cluster.

Perianth. The combined calyx and corolla of a flower; a term used especially when the parts are not readily distinguishable. See illustration, page 163.

Perfect flower. A flower with both stamens and pistils. See illustration, page 163.

Petiole. The stalk of a leaf.

Pinnate. A compound leaf in which the leaflets arise on each side of a common axis. An odd-pinnate leaf has an odd terminal leaflet. See **Bipinnate.**

Pistil. The female part of a flower, comprising ovary, style, and stigma.

Pistillate. Having pistils but no stamens.

Pith. The spongy tissue in the stem of a plant.

Pod. A dry fruit that splits open along 2 sutures. The fruits of Fabaceae (Pea family). See **Dehiscent.**

Pome. A fleshy fruit, such as the apple, composed of an outer fleshy layer and a central core with seeds enclosed in a capsule.

Pubescent. Covered with soft, short hairs.

Raceme. An unbranched, indeterminate inflorescence in which the flowers are borne in short pedicels along a central axis. See illustration, page 163.

Ray flower. An asymmetrical flower usually located at the margin of the head of plants belonging to Asteraceae (Sunflower family). The corolla appears to be a single long, narrow petal. See **Disk Flower.**

Reflexed. Abruptly bent backward or downward.

Repand. Having a slightly wavy surface or margin.

opposite leaves

palmate venation

palmate lobes

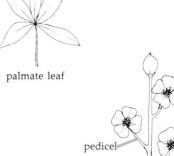

palmate leaf

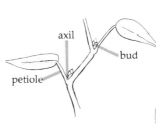

pedicel

peduncle

axil

bud

petiole

pinnate leaf

pod

pome

ray flower

Rhizome. A usually horizontal underground stem that produces leafy shoots above and roots below.

Rhizomatous. Having horizontal rhizomes that grow partially or completely beneath the soil surface.

Rhombic leaf. 4-sided leaf shaped somewhat like a diamond.

Saggitate leaf. Leaf shaped like an arrowhead, with the basal lobes pointing downward.

Sepal. One of the segments of a calyx. See illustration, page 163.

Serrate leaf. Saw-toothed leaf, with the teeth pointing forward or toward the apex.

Sessile. Without a stalk.

Simple leaf. A leaf that is not compound (divided into leaflets).

Spike. An elongated inflorescence in which the flowers are sessile along the axis. See illustration, page 163.

Spur. A tubular or saclike extension of a petal or other floral organ, usually containing a nectary.

Stamen. The pollen-bearing organ of a seed plant, typically consisting of an anther and a filament. See illustration, page 163.

Staminate. Having stamens but no pistils.

Stigma. The portion of a flower pistil that receives pollen grains and on which they germinate. See illustration, page 163.

Stipulate. Having stipules. See **Stipule**.

Stipule. Either of a pair of lateral appendages at the base of a leaf.

Stolon. A horizontal stem that runs along the ground and roots at the nodes, producing new plants.

Stoloniferous. Bearing stolons.

Style. An extension of the ovary that bears a stigma at its apex. See illustration, page 163.

Subtend. To occupy an adjacent and lower position to another structure and often enclosing it, as a bract subtending a flower.

Succulent. Thickened, fleshy tissues with varying degrees of softness.

Terminal. At the tip.

Ternate. Divided into 3 parts, as of leaves. See **Biternate**.

Tetraploid. 4 sets (twice the basic number) of chromosomes per cell. See **Diploid** and **Triploid**.

Triploid. 3 sets of chromosomes per cell. See **Diploid** and **Tetraploid**.

Umbel. An indeterminate, usually flat-topped or convex inflorescence in which the pedicels of the flowers arise from a common point, resembling the framework of an umbrella. See illustration, page 163.

Tuber. A thickened, short underground stem, as in the potato.

Whorl. Arrangement of 3 or more leaves or buds at a node.

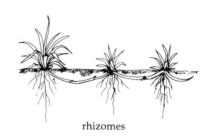

rhizomes

saggitate leaf

serrate leaf

simple leaf

stipules

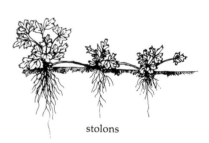

stolons

ternate leaf

Flowers

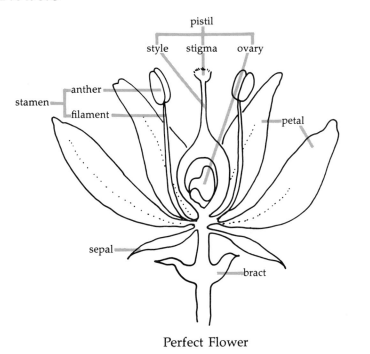

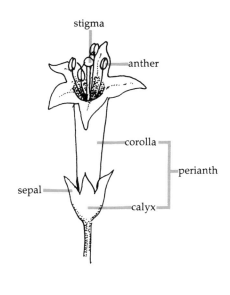

Perfect Flower

Tubular-shaped Flower

Inflorescence

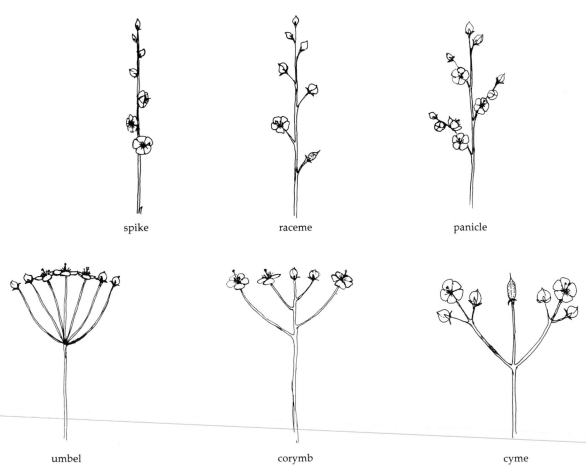

spike

raceme

panicle

umbel

corymb

cyme

Woody Ground Covers
Botanical Names of Plants

170

172

References

The publications listed below provide additional information about ground-cover plants. You can also obtain assistance from your county Cooperative Extension office, state land-grant university, the U.S. Department of Agriculture, and nationally recognized arboretums and botanical gardens.

Atkinson, Robert E. *The Complete Book of Groundcovers.* New York: David McKay Company, 1970.

Bailey, Liberty Hyde. *The Cultivated Conifers in North America.* New York: Macmillan Publishing Company, 1948.

Bailey, Liberty Hyde. *The Standard Cyclopedia of Horticulture.* 3 vols. New York: Macmillan Publishing Company, 1914.

Bean, W. J. *Trees and Shrubs Hardy in the British Isles.* 8th ed. 3 vols. London: John Murray, Ltd., 1973.

Cravens, Richard H. *Vines.* Alexandria, Virginia: Time-Life Books, Inc., 1979.

Crockett, James Underwood. *Evergreens.* New York: Time-Life Books, Inc., 1971.

Crockett, James Underwood. *Lawns and Groundcovers.* New York: Time-Life Books, Inc., 1972.

Crockett, James Underwood. *Perennials.* Alexandria, Virginia: Time-Life Books, Inc., 1972.

Cumming, Roderick W., and Robert E. Lee. *Contemporary Perennials.* New York: Macmillan Publishing Company, 1960.

Degraaf, Richard M., and Gretchen M. Witman. *Trees, Shrubs, and Vines for Attracting Birds.* Amherst, Massachusetts: University of Massachusetts Press, 1979.

Dirr, Michael A. *Manual of Woody Landscape Plants: Their Identification, Ornamental Characteristics, Culture, Propagation, and Uses.* Champaign, Illinois: Stipes Publishing Company, 1977.

Foley, Daniel J. *Groundcovers for Easier Gardening.* New York: Dover Publishers, 1972.

Giles, F. A., Rebecca McIntosh Keith, and Donald C. Saupe. *Herbaceous Perennials.* Reston, Virginia: Reston Publishing Company, 1980.

Giles, F. A., and W. B. Siefert. *Pruning and Care of Evergreen and Deciduous Trees and Shrubs.* Circular 1033. University of Illinois at Urbana-Champaign College of Agriculture Cooperative Extension Service, 1971.

Hebb, Robert S. *Low Maintenance Perennials.* New York: Quadrangle/
New York Times Book Company, 1975.

Hortus Third. Staff of the L. H. Bailey Hortorium. Cornell University.
New York: Macmillan Publishing Company, 1978.

Keith, Rebecca McIntosh, and F. A. Giles. *Dwarf Shrubs for the Midwest.*
Special Publication 60. University of Illinois at Urbana-Champaign
College of Agriculture, 1980.

Nelson, William R., Jr. *Landscaping Your Home.* Circular 1111. Rev. ed.
University of Illinois at Urbana-Champaign College of Agriculture Cooperative Extension Service, 1975.

Nelson, William R., Jr. *Planting Design: A Manual of Theory and Practice.*
Champaign, Illinois: Stipes Publishing Company, 1979.

Oudon, Pieter den, and B. K. Boom. *Manual of Cultivated Conifers.* The
Hague, Netherlands: Martinus Nijhoff, 1965.

Pirone, P. P. *Diseases and Pests of Ornamental Plants.* 4th ed. New York:
Ronald Press Company, 1970.

Still, Steven. *Herbaceous Ornamental Plants.* Champaign, Illinois: Stipes
Publishing Company, 1980.

Welch, H. J. *Dwarf Conifers.* London: Faber and Faber, 1968.

Wyman, Donald. *Dwarf Shrubs.* New York: Macmillan Publishing Company, 1975.

Wyman, Donald. *Ground Cover Plants.* New York: Macmillan Publishing Company, 1956.